P9-DWO-264

BRAIDING RAWHIDE HORSE TACK

CALGARY PUBLIC LIBRARY

MAY — - 2014

COLLEGE OF PHARMACY

MAY 1 9 2011

Braiding Rawhide Horse Tack

2nd EDITION

Robert L. Woolery

Cornell Maritime Press
A Division of
Schiffer Publishing, Ltd.
Atglen, Pennsylvania

Other Schiffer Books on Related Subjects:
Leather Care Compendium: For Shoes, Clothing, and Furniture,
978-0-7643-4517-3, $34.99
Encyclopedia of Rawhide and Leather Braiding,
978-0-87033-161-9, $29.99
Braiding Fine Leather: Techniques of the Australian Whipmakers,
978-0-87033-544-0, $19.95

Published by Schiffer Publishing, Ltd., 2013; *Braiding Rawhide Horse Tack*
was originally published by Cornell Maritime Press, Inc. in 1985.
Copyright © Cornell Maritime Press, Inc., 1985; copyright © by Robert L. Woolery, 2013.

Library of Congress Control Number: 2013940245

All rights reserved. No part of this work may be reproduced or used in any form or by any means—graphic, electronic, or mechanical, including photocopying or information storage and retrieval systems—without written permission from the publisher.

The scanning, uploading, and distribution of this book or any part thereof via the Internet or via any other means without the permission of the publisher is illegal and punishable by law. Please purchase only authorized editions and do not participate in or encourage the electronic piracy of copyrighted materials.
"Schiffer," "Schiffer Publishing, Ltd. & Design," and the "Design of pen and inkwell" are registered trademarks of Schiffer Publishing, Ltd.

Designed by Justin Watkinson • Cover by Bruce Waters
Type set in NewBskvll BT / Zurich BT

ISBN: 978-0-87033-629-4
Printed in China

Published by Schiffer Publishing, Ltd.
4880 Lower Valley Road
Atglen, PA 19310
Phone: (610) 593-1777; Fax: (610) 593-2002
E-mail: Info@schifferbooks.com

For our complete selection of fine books on this and related subjects,
please visit our website at **www.schifferbooks.com**. You may also write for a free catalog.

This book may be purchased from the publisher. Please try your bookstore first.

We are always looking for people to write books on new and related subjects.
If you have an idea for a book, please contact us at proposals@schifferbooks.com

Schiffer Publishing's titles are available at special discounts for bulk purchases for sales promotions or premiums. Special editions, including personalized covers, corporate imprints, and excerpts can be created in large quantities for special needs. For more information, contact the publisher.

In Europe, Schiffer books are distributed by
Bushwood Books
6 Marksbury Ave.
Kew Gardens
Surrey TW9 4JF England
Phone: 44 (0) 20 8392 8585; Fax: 44 (0) 20 8392 9876
E-mail: info@bushwoodbooks.co.uk
Website: www.bushwoodbooks.co.uk

This book is dedicated to all the rawhide braiders of countless generations who shared, taught, and helped those who followed.

A special thanks to my wife, Kathy, for her love, inspiration, and support. To my sons, Jeffrey and Jonathan, may this book be a lasting example that you can do anything.

CONTENTS

INTRODUCTION

This book is presented with two goals in mind. The first is to make a step-by-step presentation for the novice braider. The second is to record for posterity the various steps that were used by the makers of rawhide horse tack. Because there are still braiders in this and other countries who are trying to make a living at rawhide braiding, we will not be going into fancy or collector types of braiding. For the individual who wishes to obtain that quality of work, we will be glad to make referrals. After reading this book and seeing the amount of time and effort that goes into each piece, the reader should be in a better position to appreciate the labor involved and the price that the work of these artists deserves.

This book is aimed at allowing the reader to make his own cowboy horse tack. One old cowboy called this "bunkhouse work." Every effort has been made to make the steps as simple as possible. The reader should never assume that the steps presented here are the last word or the only way of doing the work. The goal is to allow the reader to advance in a logical and organized progression from start to finish.

There is a beauty in the simplicity, patterns, and workmanship of handmade items. Rawhide has a feel and a "life" that cannot be reproduced in man-made materials. It is the perfect example of "human ingenuity in adapting natural things to man's use." (This is one of the definitions of "art" in *Webster's Seventh New Collegiate Dictionary*.)

For this book, the author prefers to take the position of being a reporter. Though I have done some braiding and have tried what I report, the bulk of my information comes from other braiders. A big help came from a letter written by a braider who died before I had the chance to meet him, but, alas, I was also able to obtain a collection of notes that he had started to write. He is mentioned and his work is pictured in Bruce Grant's *Encyclopedia of Rawhide and Leather*

Braiding. Though I never knew him, I have been inspired by, and hereby, thank the late Ernie Ladouceur of Madera, California. Another big aid has been the personal help and teaching of Bill Dorrance from Salinas, California. This cowboy still uses a rawhide reata and makes his own tack. These men were friends and helped one another with techniques and designing tools. Another source of support has been the many members of the now-defunct Rawhide and Leather Braider's Association, organization I had founded in 1983.

One member, Mike Pollard of Dos Palos, California, writes:

> I am 81 years old and started to learn to make cowboy horse gear when I was 12 years old, around Elko, Nevada. At that time cowboys or buckaroos as they were called did not get much wages. There was no radio, television, and very little source of amusement, or way to kill time. There was always some one who knew how to work rawhide and there was always a few hides hanging on the fence as the ranchers always done there own butchering. You could sell a 60 foot reata for $12 to $15.00. Reins and Rommel for $8 or $10. Bosals from $3.50 to $5.00 depending on size and number of strands or strings. Quirts $2.00 to $3.00. If you could turn out a few articles a month you could supplement your meager income of $40-$45. Lots of the Indians were good rawhide men as well as the old Mexican vaqueros and some of the transplanted Texas and Montana cowboys I worked with.... I talked to an old boy in Idaho a few years ago in regards to this and he said, "Did you ever see a rawhider that had enough education to write a letter to any one about rawhide; or did you ever see one who had made enough money to go any distance to a meeting to show his work?"

With the help of some people who have written or talked about their ideas, we are ready to help you learn about rawhide and braiding.

1. PREPARATION OF THE HIDE

Green Hide
When cowboys are asked about rawhide, the most often quoted statement is that the best rawhide comes from an animal that "starved to death." This idea was important in the days of the rawhide reata, but is not as critical for other horse tack. The idea is that extra fat makes the rawhide soft and weak. If the braider is interested in making reins, then this would be less of a concern and some fat on the animal might even result in a better finished product. From elk to longhorn cattle, all types of hides can be used. Emie Ladouceur wrote the following in 1954:

> The worst hides are from a fat beef type animal...I don't like beef hides at all. But no hide is good for rawhide unless the animal is very thin. A thin old shelly cow has a good hide full of "glue," cuts easily, slick showing, edge that looks like glass, and the dried hide is almost transparent. I like a hide of solid color except white and no more of those for me. They seem to lack life and are poor to work. Jersey hides are best. Guernsey hides are good. Holstein hides are poor except a black Holstein-Jersey cross, if from a thin animal, then it's good. Some Brahmas are good as are some beef hides if from some thin animals. One reason I don't like a beef hide even if from a thin animal is that the back is thick and the sides thinner. Thus, they take some splitting. Where-ever you split, you're making thin string and you take something out of it.

The hide should be pulled off the animal. It is best not to use a knife to "dissect," as this can cause nicks. The skinning process starts with a cut around the neck and a cut down the belly. It is not a very pleasant job. Some ranchers will tie the dead animal to a tree and (with a rope tied through slits in the neck hide) pull the hide off with a saddle horse. A more modern way is to use a chain fastened to the bumper of a truck.

It is best to remove the hide while the animal is still warm. Delay may result in the blood pooling to the ground side. This will cause a blood clot color to the rawhide which ruins the color and quality of the hide. If you are near water, wash the hide to remove excess blood and "juices." Otherwise spread the hide out or nail it to a fence. Probably the best choice would be a location in the shade.

The hide in the following pictures was originally nailed to a fence. Then a day or two later it was placed on a shed tin roof in the shade. When I went to pick it up, it was still somewhat soft and I was able to get it into a plastic bag for the trip home. This hide had been off the animal for a number of days and thus needed to be washed and left in water for almost a full day before going on to the next step. If the hide you have is "warm" and has not dried any, then only wash it until the water runs off clear. Mike Pollard tells about an old dry hide that had hung on a fence all winter: "The magpies had picked all the flesh and tallow off." To soften that dry a hide requires two or three days in a creek with some rocks on it to weigh it down. The whole idea in this step is to get the rawhide evenly soft and ready for the next step.

Drying

Some old braiders prefer to cut the hide into string before the hair is removed. The instructions that are presented here will have the hide stretched and dried before the hair is removed. To do the proper stretching will require some materials and preparation. As wet rawhide dries it gets smaller, and this shrinking can create a great deal of force. That is why rawhide was often used in the early days when there were no nails. Rafters in adobe buildings, chairs, and even pack saddles (to name a few) were held together with rawhide (Fig. 1).

To build the frame in the photograph, I obtained five pieces of lumber. Each of these two-by-fours was 8 feet long (1-1/2 inches x 3-1/2 inches x 8 feet) stud fir. If you plan to have very large hides, then you may wish to use 10- or 12-foot lengths. The design here is intended to be the simplest design. For a stronger variation one more piece of lumber would be needed.

Using a saw, I cut a notch in the ends of four of these pieces of lumber. Then the fifth piece was cut into four brace pieces. These were then nailed together as shown in the picture. A stronger variation would use drilled holes and bolts to hold the pieces together and, using eight brace pieces as four pairs, the brace pieces would be bolted to both sides of the frame.

Next you will need from twenty-eight to thirty-six heavy S hooks. These can be either 2-inch or 2-1/2-inch. In the photographs, I used thirty-three hooks. For the amount of rope needed, allow some extra for the smaller hides. In the photograph there is 120 feet of 1/2-inch rope. I find the 2-1/2-inch hooks faster to hook onto this size rope, but both will work. These hooks can be found in a hardware store.

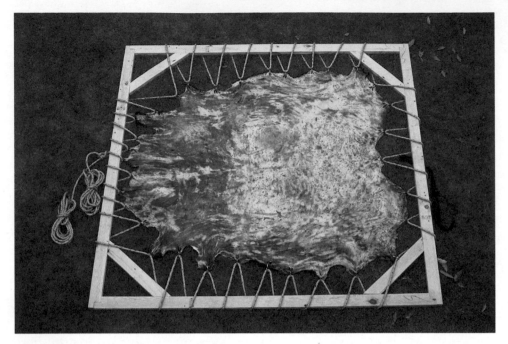

Fig. 1. The hide is placed in the frame, hair side down, and stretched tightly.

Position the frame on a clean area. The photograph shows the frame flat on a grass lawn. Now spread the hide inside the frame. The hair side should be down and the flesh side up. If you were staking the hide to the ground and not using a frame, the hide would still start with the hair side down. In that case, you would want to be in the shade and use iron stakes, 50-penny spikes, or tent pegs.

Pull the tail on the hide toward the center of one side of the frame. Then pull the opposite side of the hide. Take a very sharp knife and cut off the tail. Then using the knife, make three parallel slits in the following manner: start the cuts about 1-1/2 inches in from the edge, go about 2 inches into the hide, and space them about 1/2 inch apart. These three cuts will form two short strips that can be taken and crossed. Through the center formed when these two strips cross, insert one of the S hooks. The results should look like the photograph (Fig. 2). This step will be repeated each time a hook is to be placed. This way the hooks will not tear through as the hide dries.

Put hooks in the tail area and the center of the neck. Then put one in each of the four legs. Follow this with three on each side between the front and hind legs. Once you have placed these first dozen hooks, go ahead and attach the rope as pictured. Simply go around the wood frame, through a hook, around the frame, through a hook, etc. Then pull out all the slack in the rope.

At this point you can now see where additional hooks will be needed. With the rope still tight, go around and attach the additional hooks to the hide. (If you need a reference, try using about 14 inches for spacing of the

Fig. 2. An example of how the hook should be placed into the hide. This picture was taken after the hide had dried.

hooks.) Then remove the rope from the original dozen hooks. Start the rope this time with the first hook at the head end. Make sure you go through each hook and around the frame for every hook all the way around the hide. Once this is done, start at the tail end and remove all the slack in the rope. This is probably easiest with two people staying even with each other but working around the opposite sides of the hide. The theory is that the hide should be stretched the same as it was on the animal. If one person is doing this, he should tighten one or two passes on one side and then move and tighten the corresponding ones on the opposite side. Try to keep the hide centered in the frame and not pulled more to one side than the other.

With a large hide, stretch as tight as possible. Sometimes this causes the "juice" to come out of the hide. A calf hide can be stretched in a frame made of 1 -inch pipe. Also one can use baling wire in place of the rope. The advantage of the wire is that it does not stretch. Some people use iron stakes that measure 3/4 inch thick and about 2 feet long.

The frame should be placed in the shade. If shade is not available, then cover the hide with canvas so that the sun will not burn the hide. I prefer to lean the frame against a convenient wall or fence. After a short period of drying, take a round-end skinning knife or D-shaped leather knife and remove any excess fat from the tissue side. This is not a cutting motion! Use the tool perpendicular to the hide and scrape with parallel strokes. Excess fat could make soft places.

Dry for two or three days if the weather is warm. In average weather, one week is probably necessary. It may be a good idea to take a garden rake or broom and brush the hair side. This will sweep out a lot of dirt and raise up any matted hair. Either heavy dirt or matted hair could prevent an area from drying completely. The hide in the photographs took longer than a week due to the excess fat in it and some rain. In fact, the hide did not finish drying until the hair had been removed. Thus the hide will remain in the frame for the next step, which is the hair removal.

Removal of Hair

There are a number of ways of removing the hair. Everyone seems to develop his own favorite work-saving methods. Mike Pollard tells about watching Dick Martinez in 1914. His technique was to cut 5/8- to 3/4-inch wide strings (see chapter 2) with the hair still on. Then he "took the string and stretched it out on the fence, pulled it good and tight, and left it for a day or two till it was dry enough to scrape the hair off with his knife." In another description, Mike tells about watching Jim Vernon about 1923.

He had a washtub full of wood ashes which he sifted thru an old screen door. He worked the ashes into the hair with the back of the rake till there wasn't much hair showing. He took an old shovel handle, cut it to a chisel edge with a hacksaw. Smoothed it up with a file and rounded the corners so they would not gouge into the hide. He started at the backbone and worked out. The ashes braced the hair like lather braces a man's whiskers, and in about an hour he had all the hair off out to the outside stake holes.

The following is from a letter written by Ernie Ladouceur in 1954. I have talked to a lot of old "braiders" and they agree with what he says.

I might tell you that you could lime a hide to remove the hair, but you get such a poor rawhide that it isn't much good. I know men that use that process, but they never turn out good stuff. Also, you could cure a hide with lye, remove the hair, and cut the lye with a bath of vinegar and water, but it's just not good old rawhide. I make fine rawhide out of a good hide. No one can make fine rawhide out of a poor hide. I've seen a lot of poor rawhide that might have been good if it hadn't been dipped to take the hair off.

With this background, you now know why we will be removing the hair with a knife. With a small hide you can drape it over your knee and use a round-ended pocket knife. Ernie Laduceur wrote that "the old timers used to scrape a hide by putting it over a three inch pipe and scraping with one blade of a sheep shear which in those days was made of good steel." Because we are not working with strips or curved hides, we will need to use a knife that has a good curve in the design. You may wish to do this work with a knife you have or make. A good suggestion is the D-shaped leather knife that Tandy Leather Company lists as a "head knife" (#1570). The first thing to do with the knife is to sharpen it to a very good edge. Due to the dirt in the hair, you will want to stop and resharpen the knife often. Thus, a good sharpening stone or grindstone is a must.

With a little practice you will find the proper angle to hold the knife. Basically the blade is close to perpendicular to the hide. You will use good long strokes to scrape off the hair. Scrape with the slope of the hair and not against it. You may wish to vary your strokes for a while at about five or ten degrees to one side of how the hair grows. Then change to about five or ten degrees to the opposite side of how the hair grows. It will not take long to develop a feel for when the strokes work best. Be careful not to cut too deep and take too much of the surface or "grain" off the hide. Those areas that will be cut out and discarded do not have to be dehaired. As I mentioned earlier, once the hair is removed, the rawhide might be able to dry even further (Fig. 3).

Fig. 3. My wife finished the job of scraping hair off the dry hide.

2. FABRICATING THE STRINGS

Initial Cutting

This section is called initial cutting because we will be cutting a string that will then be further refined into the final strings. Before we start any string cutting, though, there are a couple of preparatory steps. First move the frame so that you can get behind it with sunlight on the opposite side. Then look for grubs, holes, light spots, large scars, and any other bad spots that you do not want in your final strings. These undesirable spots should be cut out of the hide. There will be some small defects that can be left for a later step if you wish.

Now the hide can be cut from the frame. Because the neck, flank, and some of the tail are of no value, the cut can remove these undesired sections. In the drawing I have shown Mr. Ladouceur's ideas concerning what portion of the hide is good for what type of work. Also remember that the type of work depends on the hide being considered. Thus there is not just one best way to cut a hide.

At this point we can again refer to Ernie Ladouceur's 1954 letter. A drawing that explains his description is pictured in Fig. 4.1 made one from a broom handle (Fig. 7). A hammer handle would make a larger and probably stronger version. An extra nail can be used to go through the hole in the razor blade if the blade starts to slip. After the large hide is real dry—Bone Dry—I pull the stakes and trim the stuff that is no good. [See drawings.]

> The sketch is not in proportion at all but maybe you get the idea of the kinds of rawhide in a hide. They are different and should be used for different purposes. The part that I marked "best rawhide" is a large egg shaped piece. Out of a large green hide I generally get a 400-foot piece about ½-inch wide. A hundred feet from the two front pieces (50 feet each) and about 50 feet out of the rump two pieces. The larger piece I cut around making a string about ½-inch wide. The neck and rump I cut about 3/8 inch wide. [See Fig. 5.]

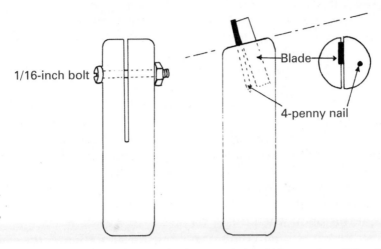

Fig. 4. The hand tool. The cut or slot in the wood should be made a little off center, so that the inside edge is through the middle. The 4-penny nail (you can cut its head off) should be halfway into the wood. The cutting edge of the blade is in the center, and the blade itself has a slight tilt. It is a wise idea to dull the top and exposed corners of the blade. Besides the consideration of your safety, you will not cut the hide if the tool slips under the hide when cutting.

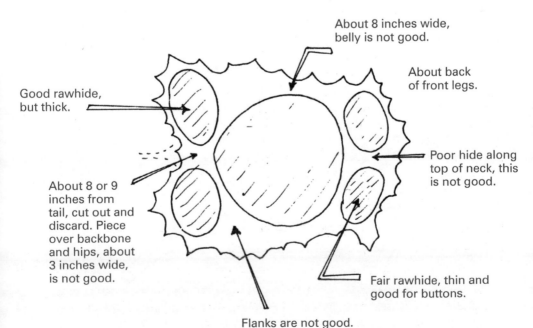

Fig. 5. Parts of the hide.

After the hides are scraped, I wet them "good" until partly soft. Then cover them with wet or damp (only) sacks until the moisture is about uniform throughout, and just moist enough to cut good. Then I cut them up into sections, as I mentioned, and then stretch the moist strings.

It's no use to leave any poor stuff in your string as it will just spoil your work. If you cut the hide up in a wide string and stretch it, you won't have a good string. Part will stretch and part won't. Then when you braid, one pulls down and the other won't. If you cut a hide up with a wide cut, say 1-1/2 inches and you cut around, you get something like this. [See Fig. 6.] Now when you stretch it, the inside gets all the stretch and the outside none. If you cut it a ½-inch wide, you get a good stretch across the string. When cutting the hide into strings, don't try to make too square a turn. Trim off enough at the sharp turn to keep it reasonably round, otherwise the piece may break at this point when it is stretched.

All these pieces are put in water for about 1/2 hour. Before the water has gone through the hide, I take the pieces out and shake the excess water off. Then I wrap them in moist sacks long enough so that no part is wet but all parts are moist throughout. The less water used on rawhide the better. They should be about moist enough to braid with only.

I made some knives to cut around the sections with and they are fast and good. With just a little practice you can cut a large hide into a long string and it will be uniform and pretty. I took some pieces of broom handle and shaped them like this. [See Fig. 7.]

I made several of these knives, some for heavy hides and a wide cut; and some for light skins and a narrow cut. The knife I use for heavy hides takes

Too sharp an angle is not good.

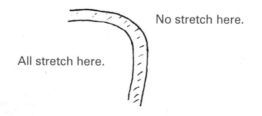

No stretch here.

All stretch here.

It is better to trim off some of the corner.

Fig. 6. Too sharp an angle is not good; it is better to trim off some of the corner.

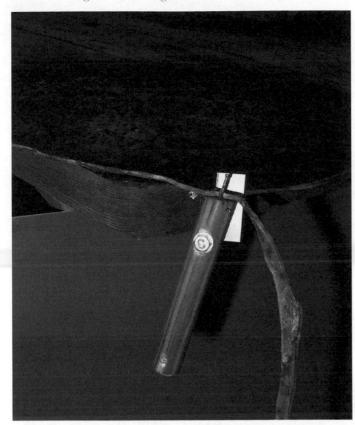

Fig. 7. Here we are making the first cut for strings. The strip is not even, so we are going to cut it wider than our desired width.

about 1/2-inch cut and less for lighter hides. Experience will be the guide. If you cut them too narrow, they will pull down in being stretched and may be too narrow for much use. If in doubt, cut them a little wide. They are sure to narrow down on being stretched.

These knives that I made to cut around the hide are made so that the blade is pointed toward the man when the handle is held also pointing toward the man. On light hides I use a slick razor blade. On heavy hides I make a short blade out of a piece of "high speed" common hacksaw blade. Put the hide on a table with the piece being cut extending over the edge. Start your cut and as you pull or hold the cut string with your left hand, hold the hide from moving with your left elbow. The knife should be just slightly in back of the center of the nail or pin for best cutting. A little practice is all that is necessary. Use the knife so that the handle has an easy angle toward you and the blade has a slight angle against the cut. It's fast and easy. Don't try to move the hide while cutting. In working rawhide or leather, the relation between the position of the pin and the knife is important. Usually the edge of the knife should be at the center of the pin for best results. But, in cutting around the hide, I have found that the cutting edge is slightly behind the center of the pin. This way it is easier to cut around with less likelihood of cutting the string off.

If you study the drawings you will see that the blade is tipped forward at about a fifteen- to twenty-degree angle. I feel that this is an important fact here and, later, with the string cutting tool. The theory is that the cutting action of the blade tends to push the hide down onto the handle. You might compare this to the angle that one uses when sawing wood with a hand saw.

You may also find an advantage in pulling the newly cut string away from the hide by about twenty degrees. This tends to keep the hide against the nail and thus keep the thickness more consistent.

Another suggestion is to use your D-shaped knife or head knife to cut the more even curves that were suggested above. This knife on a hard surface does a very good job if it is kept very sharp.

Once the string is cut, it should be stored in a coil about 30 inches in diameter. Be careful not to make any sharp bends, twists, or kinks in it, as this might cause cracks in the grain. Tie some string in three or four places to keep the coils in place.

The next step is to rehumidify the rawhide strings. This can be done by putting them back in water. The better way would be to cover them with damp rags or sacks overnight or for 6 to 12 hours.

Preparation of Strings

For these steps, you will need two pieces of equipment. The first one is a flesher to skive the strips to an even and consistent thickness. The simplest flesher can be made with a wooden log or a large block of wood. Into this wood cut a large notch. The bottom of the notch can be lined with metal from a tin can which can be nailed in place. Then a "mowing machine section," a blade from a large wood plane, can be hammered down across the notch. The space between the blade and the metal lining will determine the thickness of the rawhide. Improved variations are demonstrated in the photographs. In one example (Fig. 8), the blade can swing one direction to aid in placing the strip of rawhide. In a fancier version of the tool, the flesher consists of a planer blade. The surface that the rawhide is drawn across does not rotate. It is pivoted on an off-center axle and can be locked in place. Thus, thickness of the cut is changed by moving the roller-like surface. A low gap can be left in the lower right corner to start string through.

The second tool you will need is the string cutter. It can be very simple or very complicated. The simplest string cutter is a very sharp pocket knife hammered into a block of wood. In Fig. 9 there is an example of just such an arrangement. This particular one was used by Bill Dorrance while stationed aboard a ship during World War II. His present tools have thumbscrews for very small adjustments (Fig. 10). He prefers to use an old straight razor for the blade. Because the blade is hollow-ground, he feels that there is less pull or friction. Since the sharpening of such a blade is almost an art in itself, many today will tend to stick to disposable, single-edge razor blades; but they must be blades that have some thickness and strength. Industrial-quality blades on up to the blades for utility knives will all do fine. The main caution with all of these blades is to be very careful. Such sharp blades can cut you before you are even aware that you have touched the blade.

Fig. 8. Made by Fred Dorrance (Bill's brother) and marked "May 1993," this is a splitter made from a wood-plane blade, used by Bill Dorrance of Salinas, California. When used, it is held in a vise. The blade can be swiveled to allow the string to be placed and started.

Fig. 9. A pocket knife and a notched piece of wood made a simple tool that Bill Dorrance once used.

Fig. 10. These are Bill Dorrance's string cutters: the top one for straight cuts and the bottom one for bevels. They allow for making fine adjustments by turning the knob. Bill uses a straight razor blade in both of these tools.

The fancier string cutters employ simply a vise to hold the blade and a guide surface. Some people prefer to use two blades separated by a spacer of known width to cut the smaller strings. These instructions will be limited to the use of one blade. The cutting of strings will go smoothly and easily with an extremely sharp blade.

Earlier I mentioned the importance of the blade angle. The easiest way that I have found to explain this is to suggest the comparison with a hand saw cutting wood. If you picture the angle at which a saw cuts wood, you will see that it is not a 90-degree angle to the surface of the wood. If the blade were positioned at a 90-degree angle to the rawhide, there would be a tendency for the softer areas to bunch up on the blade. Now for comparison, angle the blade so that it cuts the top surface before it cuts the bottom surface. This angle will have the effect of pushing the material down onto the guide surface. Thus the material is actually being cut between the blade and the guide surface rather than being pulled squarely against the blade.

Now let's take our softened rough-cut strings from the earlier section and turn them into strings ready for braiding. The first step is to get the fibers set into more of a straight line. Tie one end to a fence post. Then go out 50 or 150 feet, and around another post. Continue around, pulling the string fairly tight until all of it is used. For one person, this may take 1-1/2 hours. If two people are working at this, it may take only 1/2-hour. (I recently heard the suggestion of using a smooth, long log to wrap the rawhide around rather than going out straight.) This particular step is one that some braiders elect to omit. Some feel that the excess stretching causes a tearing of fibers and a subsequent loss of "life" in the rawhide.

Let the string dry. As before, this may take a couple of days and is best done in the shade. We have now gone from string cut in a rough circle to a straight string. At this time, carefully go over all of the string looking for bad spots, grub holes, and such. If there are any in the center of the string, mark them on the hair side with an indelible pencil. If the flaw is near the edge, then make a knife cut that removes the area and also blends into enough of the existing edge that this change is not noticeable. Now take the string down and coil it up. As before, be careful not to make any sharp bends.

Put the string in water for 3 or 4 minutes and then cover with damp sacks or rags for 12 hours. If there are large variations in the string width, you may wish to run the string through the cutter to get a more consistent width. At this point we are ready to start the string through the flesher blade (Fig. 11). Because the hide varies in thickness, do not set the blade too low for the first run-through. Too low a setting will make it too hard to pull. Be sure not to allow the scraps, or fleshing, to collect around the blade. Such a build-up could make you cut the string off or make thin areas. A good suggestion is to use some dry rags or burlap to remove the excess moisture and fleshing. Again be careful not to cut yourself when removing these

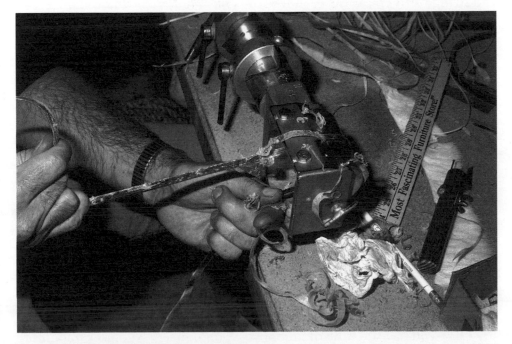

Fig. 11. Splitting the string to an even thickness. This tool was made by Frank Hansen of Lakeview, Oregon. Note that some fat made the scrap strip darker than the good part of the string. Caution! When removing excess fat and "juices" that build up near the blade, do not use your fingers! A very sharp blade will cut you without your even feeling it.

excesses. If you are not on a clean floor, then you may wish to place burlap, canvas, or plastic around your work area to keep the string out of the dirt. Experience will show you how and where to hold the wet string with your left hand while pulling with your right hand. (As rawhide is very hard on the hands, you may wish to use old gloves.)

Once you have the string to the desired thickness, the next step is to gauge for width. One point that is worth stressing here concerns the thickness to which you may wish to trim your rawhide. The rule of thumb is to thin only to equal your thinnest area. Thus the thickness of the hide will determine the type of items that you wish to make. If you plan to cut strings of only 1 or 2 millimeters width, then you should be using newborn calf hide. For a reata, the plaits could easily be at least 1/8-inch thick and over ¼-inch wide. Just do not expect to take reata-quality rawhide and transform it into miniature strings by thinning.

If your string has dried out, you will have to rehumidify it to an even dampness. Find the last end of the original spiral string. With the guide edge on the left and the blade adjusted to the desired width on the right, start your string with the hair side up. This should place the straightest side next to the guide edge. (Better sections of the trim strip can be saved for smaller knots or core material.) Make this first cut a small amount wider than you wish to have the finished string. Go the full length of your string. Adjust the blade to the desired final width. Now take the last end and once more take the string through for the total length. The rule here is that the edge that has the most recent cut will be the edge that goes against the guide surface.

Once the string is cut to the desired even width, the blade will be adjusted to a 45-degree angle for beveling. The width for the guide surface will have to be adjusted by trial and error, so use a short 4 or 5 feet of your string to test the adjustment. First we will remove a slight corner of the flesh or skived side. Adjust so that your cut will be as shown in the drawing. Run it all the way through for one side and then repeat for the other side. Then re-adjust your settings to take a larger corner off the hair side (Fig. 12). Go the full length and repeat for the last corner or edge. Note that for very small strings, you may not wish to bevel the edges. Also, many braiders do not bevel the flesh side. The idea here is that you will get a less fuzzy string this way. Some braiders take too much off with their beveling in order to make the strings look smaller than they really are. You should also be aware that with leather, the bevel is only on the flesh side. (In David Morgan's Whips and Whipmaking, there is a suggestion to bevel alternate corners with small leather strings. Thus there is much room for variation. I even know of a braider who does very nice and very fine work without beveling any of the corners.) Much of the strength is in the hair side of the string, so try not to get too carried away with beveling. (See Fig. 13.)

Once you have done all of the above, you will need to go back once more and look for bad spots in the string. Remember, most were marked earlier with indelible pencil. If you are going to make a four-plait reata, you will be trying to get at least four long strings (try for 90 feet each) out of what you have prepared. Before you make any cuts, shift the string around trying to keep all the bad spots near one end. Thus you will make a zigzag pattern with the string. The bend will be where you make a cut, so move the bends around to the best advantage. This is a little easier with shorter projects where the bad spots can be removed and only good sections of the proper length are used. A suggested length then would be 60 feet. Twelve- to fifteen-foot strings are used for the button knots.

Once the strings are cut to the desired lengths, they should be rolled in "tamales." It is suggested that you start in the center, thus making two rolls out of each string. This rawhide can be hung on a nail and left to dry until just before it's needed for braiding. At that time, you will have to rehumidify the strings as described earlier. Usually about half an hour in damp sacks will be enough. The trick is to have the rawhide at just the right moisture content for braiding. Most beginners will get the rawhide too wet. This judgment call will probably be the hardest thing to learn in all your working with rawhide.

Fig. 12. Taking off the corner. Once the corner is removed for the full length of the string, repeat the process for the other corner. Bevel the hair-side corners of rawhide; bevel the flesh-side corners of leather. Do not bevel too much, since much of the strength of the string is in the hair side of the rawhide.

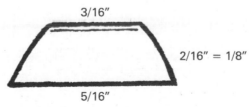

Fig. 13. A reata string.

3. INTRODUCTION TO PLAITS

The term "plait" can be used as a verb meaning "to braid." It can also be used to describe "a braid." In this work we will use the term to help describe round, squared, or rope-like lengths of braiding. Terms such as "four-plait" will be used to explain that the length of braiding is made by continued interlacing of four laces, strings, or thongs.

There is no limit to the number of ropes, laces, thongs, or strings that can be braided into a long rope. The smallest number, of course, is one. The most practical example would be a twisted core. This is made by taking a single strip of damp rawhide and twisting it until smooth. Then it is nailed down at both ends and left to dry. A core can be made using many pieces of rawhide, but we were trying to show an example of "one-plait."

For "two-plait," or braiding using only two pieces of material, the best example is a slit braid (Fig. 14). A slit braid is simply one where a small cut or slit is made lengthwise in the center of one lace. Then the other is passed through the slit and turned so that the two laces can lie flat against each other. A slit is now cut in the second lace and the first is passed through as before. This is continued for the desired length. Thus we have braided two strips together.

With "three-plait" we start to get into true braiding. This braid is often used by girls with "ponytails." Take two laces and place them parallel to each other. Take the third and lace it through the others for one over and one under. The two will be at a ninety-degree angle to the single. Now start with the top one of the set of two. Bring it over the one below it and over to be parallel to and below the one that was the single. This gives us a two and one that is opposite to where we started. Continue as before with the top of the set of two going over the one below and to the other side. This is the only odd-number braid that we will talk about. If you wish to braid five, seven, nine, and other odd numbers, the instructions are to be found in other books.

Fig. 14. A slit braid made
by Gail Hought.

The most useful braids for the beginner with rawhide are four and eight.
Then one should try six and twelve. Some braiders like to get fancy with
sixteen, thirty-two, and even more plaits. In this book we will keep things
simple. Remember that with four and eight plaits, you can make everything
in this book (Fig. 15).

Rather than presenting these braids one at a time, let us show how similar
they are. First, where there are an even number of strands, arrange them so
that half the number are on one side and half are on the other. The starting
position can be figured from the drawings. In all of these braids, the next
strand will pass behind the work. It will also return to the same side from
which it started. As one holds the braiding in a position similar to how it
is shown in the drawing, this working strand is always the first strand from
the top.

The formula for four-plait is *under one* and *over one*.
The formula for eight-plait is *under two* and *over two*.

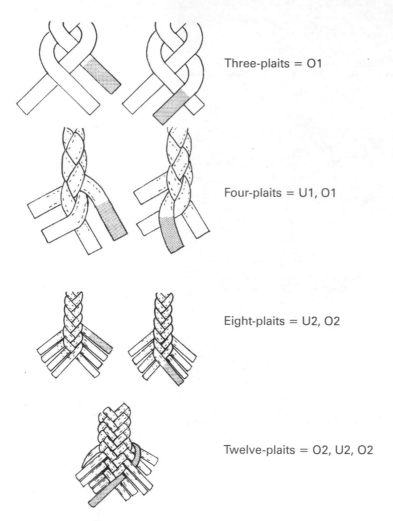

Three-plaits = O1

Four-plaits = U1, O1

Eight-plaits = U2, O2

Twelve-plaits = O2, U2, O2

Fig. 15. Sample plaits.

In the photographs we have demonstrated examples of four, six, and eight plait braids (Fig. 16). When eight-plait is done without a core, it forms a square pattern in cross section (Fig. 17). Even to this day, many riders prefer the feel of reins that are an eight-plait square. Their reasons go beyond extra stiffness from a core. It is the shape that they like. If one is trying to hold reins and throw a rope, it is nice to be able to feel more of a difference than that between reins and round rope. We will have more to say about cores later.

The six-plait is the one that might make things seem confusing. There are three types of six-strand braiding. The one that you will be least interested in is the "half round." It has a formula of under two and over one. Dave Stewart of Sonora, California, told me that he made a reata using the half-round braid. This cowboy and superb braider said that this reata would

Fig. 16. Examples of braids: left, a four-plait reata by Bill Dorrance; center, six-plait hobbles by Frank Hansen; right, eight-plait hobbles by Jack Shepard.

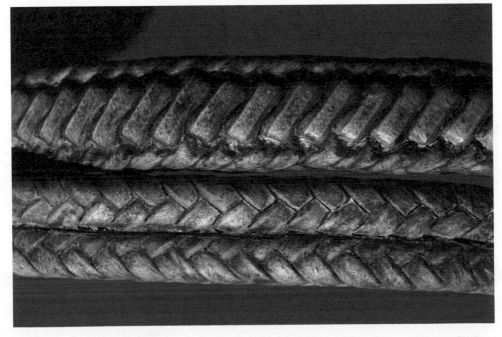

Fig. 17. Eight plait without a core. This example, part of a set of hobbles made by the late Ernie Ladouceur, shows both squared and laced together versions.

stay open easier than any he had made. It did not tend to "figure eight" the loop as most ropes do. In general, however, the half round is not used.

The small eye of a twelve-plait romal is made by using the six-plait round. By starting in the center of your lace, a short length of six-plait can be bent around and continued as twelve. For six-plait you can use the formula over one, under one, over one. The third form of six-plait has an alternating pattern to the instructions. On one side you will go under two and over one. Then on the next side you will go under one and over two.

The twelve-plait can be done two ways. One formula is under three and over three. The other is over two, under two, over two. Most of the work that I have photographed for this book uses the latter formula.

I strongly suggest that you take some material and practice these plaits before you start a project. Also, start with four- and eight-plaits for your first few projects. Once you have mastered these braids, the fancier plaits will be easier (Figs. 16 and 17).

4. INTRODUCTION TO KNOTS

There are many books that show many types of knots. In this volume, we will confine ourselves to a very limited number of knots. Our goal is to keep things simple and to try not to confuse the reader. But before we get into some of the specifics, there is a need to cover some background information.

Many of the old braiders do not "tie" a knot. Instead they "weave" or "braid" a button or knot. We will introduce this when we talk about the nose button for the bosal. Just remember that the same or related techniques can be used for many of the other knots shown. This technique does not require the use of formulas; also, interesting patterns can be created without problem. The old-timers' weave or braid technique uses many strings and starts near the middle of the strings. The idea of starting in the middle of the string can also be carried over to the single-string techniques. All you do is use one half of the string to tie the foundation knot and use the other half for the interweave.

As mentioned before, most of these instructions are based on a tied or sewn knot. This technique is probably the easiest to describe and easiest for the beginner to learn. Compare this technique to having a needle and thread with a knot tied in one end for sewing a straight line in some fabric. The end with the knot in it will pull against the fabric on the first stitch and not do anything after that. Thus we have a "dead end" and a "working end." In tying a rawhide or leather knot, it is best to have an extra length to the dead end. This extra length can be held down with your hand or temporarily tied down with some string. On the working end you will need to place a needle. Tandy Leather Company sells some "life-eye" needles for this use, or you can make your own out of aluminum pie plates or tin cans (Fig. 18). Cut a piece of metal about 2 inches long and about ½-inch wide at one end and narrower at the other. Put your lace against one inch of the longer edge.

Then either fold or roll the metal around the lace to form the shape of a tube-like needle. Using pliers, crimp the metal tight against the lace. You

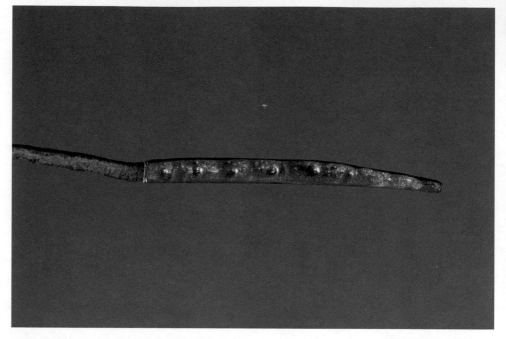

Fig. 18. This simple needle was made by Bill Dorrance out of tin can type material.

may even wish to take a nail and tap some dents into the metal to act like teeth to hold the lace in place.

The following formulas for knots require some explanation. We will take you step by step through two of the most important knots. Then we will present these instructions in the form of formulas. Following these instructions will be a generalized formula for any length of this particular knot. Because all the instructions will be aimed at this final Key to Knots, we will first give you some of the directions that apply to that page.

The goal here has been to simplify the instructions and organize the information so that, if you stop or get distracted, you will be able to find where you left off or, better yet, have a system to note where you stopped. There are some differences from other instructions which should be noted. For example, the drawings and photographs should be followed from left to right just as one reads a page. The starting point will usually be found in the upper left-hand corner of any drawing. This makes the drawings upside down from those in other books, but the working end stays where you can see it longer rather than going behind the core in the very first steps. For the novice who is trying to follow the written instructions, this should make the instructions easier to follow. The work is still done clockwise, but the orientation is rotated to aid the written page. As a result, we do not say "up" or "down" but use "A." and "B." to indicate one direction and the opposite. Thus the braider can hold his work in any position he wishes and still follow the directions.

A change of directions is called a bight. For these directions, though, we assign a number to each complete cycle. In other words, if a six-bight knot is to be tied, we number as if six strings were used. Note that each pass has a bight at the halfway point which is at the opposite end of the knot. Thus you could say that 1 .A. is the starting wrap of the lacing in a clockwise manner. When it reverses direction to return (or makes a bight), it becomes 1 .B. When it reaches its bight near the start (depending on the knot), it will become 2.A., and so forth. In this type of presentation, a resulting under two or over two will have a "+" (plus sign) to get your attention.

"U" stands for under and "O" stands for over. "U2X" means under two that form a cross. "U3X" means under two that cross and under one more adjacent. This is best seen in the drawings and photographs.

If the basic knot is to be six-bight, then the end of step six will finish the basic knot. The following interweave could be a new colored string for patterns. If you started with a long enough lace, the same one can be used. For those who look carefully, the continued use of the same string will result in a slight irregularity of the geometrical pattern. You could say that six should become one in a never-ending pattern. Speaking of ends, any time you end a plait you should try to be at a point where you can "bury under at least three" before it is cut off.

The key to these knots is presented in the following photographs and drawings. If you rotate the knots 180 degrees and refigure the formula, you would have to use more unders in the early steps. I was once told that a knot should be tied so that it does not require much in the way of going back through to tighten. As a result, these instructions are presented to take advantage of overs.

If you are using 1/8-inch lace, then the following lengths are suggested. For a small round (1/2-inch-long) button knot, use 3 feet and you should have about 4 inches remaining when finished. For a longer (1-1/2-inch-long) button knot (X = 2 in the formula), start with 6 feet and you will have about 8 inches remaining when finished. For an even longer (2-inch) button knot (X = 3 in the formula), use 8 feet and you may have about 5 inches remaining. Longer lengths are probably best done with the multiple string method.

For most of these knots, we suggest the use of 1/8-inch lace or leather string that is cut 1/8-inch wide and about 1/32-inch thick. The string should be quite flexible. If rawhide is used, the trick is to get its moisture content just right. This is best done by putting the string in a container with some moisture-producing matter. This process is called "casing," and there are several suggested techniques. One way is to wrap the string in a damp rag and leave it for several hours or overnight. Another is to put the string in a plastic bag with several drops of water and half of a raw potato. With the bag closed, the rawhide can be stored several days. Do not leave it too long or the string will get black and moldy. A third technique is to build a humidor out of an airtight container. Place some type of shelf in the container to keep the string above and out of the water. I use an inverted plastic dish or a layer of marbles. In any case, keep the strings in a humid environment but not resting in water.

In Fig. 19, you will notice a dish with an old shaving brush and a bar of white soap. Work the brush on the soap to make a lather and lightly apply the lather to the rawhide being worked. This is an instruction not to be overdone. If a little is good, then more is not better. This last step, when working with leather, is to pull the flesh side of the string over a piece of paraffin or wax once. Too much will make the string too slippery.

You will need a pick when working button knots (Fig. 20). Ernie Ladouceur wrote in his June 15, 1964, letter:

> Now the pick. This can be a nail in a wooden handle or most anything that will give you a piece of metal about two inches long and 1/8-inch in diameter. We like a pick that has the point ground flat for about an inch coming to a tapered point at the end. The point should not be sharp and we like a slight bend upward about 1/4-inch from the pointed end. A point like this seems to take less arm movement to use. The handle can be anything that you can hold easily in the palm of your hand while working with the fingers of that hand. The handle can be quite short, so long as you have good control of the point in using the pick. We use several size picks depending on the size of the string being worked.

Before we can start a button, we should say something about what the button is going over. Most of the samples are tied on wooden dowels which measure 1/2-inch in diameter. The eight-bight knot is on a 7/8-inch dowel. These were used because they were simple and kept the knot flatter for photography. In practice you will want to have a raised surface to tie over.

This "button core" will give shape to the knot and also help hold the knot in place. We must also remember that the choice of a button knot will depend on how it holds to the core. As Ernie Ladoucer wrote, "Sometimes a person will attempt to make a finer button by using a finer string and more bights until the framework collapses to the center. It would be better in such a case to use a number of bights that will hold the core well." A finer knot can be made using interweaves. This is actually getting ahead of ourselves, but is important for understanding why we are doing a procedure.

Many of the old-time rawhide men would wrap or "whip" a core of string. The problems with this technique are: it requires some time; the button will pull in from the ends; and the pick might break or snag the string. Bill Dorrance uses wood putty to make a hard button core. In the photographs we have demonstrated the cores that were under two knots on some old leather reins that are falling apart from much use (Figs. 21 and 22). These knots are described later as six-bight of one and two wraps (X = 1 and X = 2). The smaller (X = 1) was done over a simple rawhide ring knot. The

Fig. 19. Bill Dorrance's work area. Note the white cup on the right holding an old shaving brush and a bar of soap.

Fig. 20. Bill Dorrance working on some of his hobbles, May 1983.

Fig. 21. These leather reins have been used so much that some of the strings have fallen off, allowing us to see the core or foundation for the knot (left). The round knot has been built over a rawhide ring knot (right). Leather ring knots are also shown.

Fig. 22. The long knot on the reins shown in Fig. 21.

larger button was done over a core similar to what we will describe next. In a 1964 letter, Ernie Ladouceur wrote:

> Now before we start a button framework, let us say something about a core. To use a core is very important and the core should be of a material that is simple to use, easy to purchase, and will hold its shape after a button is woven over it.... We use a cloth adhesive tape that we buy at a sheet metal shop. [The tape is] either 2 inches wide or 4 inches wide and 500 feet long. It is not too expensive if you can use this quantity. I usually stick about 8 inches of this tape on a smooth painted board ... and give it a coat of lacquer or paint. I let this paint dry thoroughly and sometimes give it two coats. This stiffens the cloth so that when a button is woven tight over a core of such material, the core will hold its shape.... The paint does not allow the adhesive to ooze out through the braid as I have had unpainted tape do.... I have found three wraps of tape to be sufficient on all work except where a heavy string is to be used to weave a button. In using this tape, I put about 12 inches of it on a smooth piece of 1 inch by six inch board and cut from this the size strip I may need.

Before you start working on rawhide button knots, I strongly suggest that you do some practice buttons. The following chapters will help you get started with the basic knots. The practice knots that are pictured were made using a grained vinyl lace that is sold at Tandy Leather stores. Because only one side is textured, you can practice not twisting your lace just like you will have to do with the rawhide or leather lace.

5. FIRST KNOT

We will start with one of the most useful knots to know. This knot can be used on reins, romals, hobbles, and many other pieces. In starting this knot we will also be establishing some of the constants that we will use throughout these pages. Any knot can be tied many different ways. But in this book we will always start each knot in the same direction, namely, clockwise. Thus by wrapping your lace in a clockwise direction as shown in the photograph, you will have started any number of various knots. This particular knot is a six-bight foundation knot with a single interweave. You might say that it is a knot within a knot. If the interweave is done in a different color, you will get a pattern like that shown in the photographs.

The first step is to wrap the lace in a clockwise pattern (Fig. 23). When you are doing a small round button knot you do not have to wrap very far. In fact, once you get halfway around (180 degrees), you will start back up toward the dead end. You will cross the dead end at the start. Just remember to leave some length to the dead end to hold it down, or you can tie it down with some string. This extra length will be outside the final knot. To put these instructions into our short form, they will read as follows:

1. Make a clockwise pass—over at the start.

For the second pass we will take the lace parallel to the first pass. Allow a space equal to the width of one lace. Thus the second pass will not be tight against the first until it actually crosses. This second pass will cross the first as an over. Note that this is the second time that the lace has crossed and everything has been over this far. Now, on the way back toward the starting point, we come to our first under one, over one sequence. The description for this part of the instructions is as follows:

2A. 01 (Parallel to the first pass)
2B. U1, 01

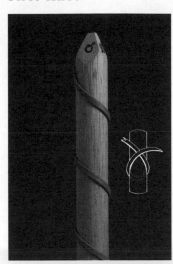

One Turn
X = 1

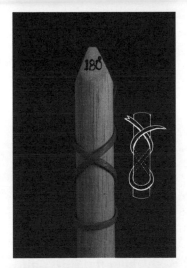

Second cross on back side
X = 2

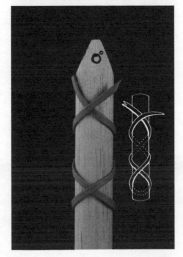

Third cross
X = 3

Fig. 23. Key to X = a number.

The third pass will contine with the under one, over one as before. In fact, there is a pattern to these instructions. The first half of any given pass will usually be a repeat of the last half of the previous pass. Returning in the second part of this pass, we have another over followed by the under, over pattern. Thus you might be tempted to say that we have under two, but they are far apart and separated by a bight. Thus we will describe this pass as:

   3. U1, 01,   01, U1, 01

The fourth pass will follow in a simple over, under pattern throughout. It will be noted:

   4. 01, U1, 01,   U1, O1, U1, O1

At this point you have tied a four-bight knot.

The fifth pass will again have the over of the first half followed by an over in the second half. The notations for number five will read:

   5. U1,01,U1,01   01,U1,01,U1,01

The sixth pass will be our final part of the six-bight foundation knot. It will be a simple over, under sequence:

   6. 01,U1,01,U1,01   U1,01,111,01,111,01

This will put you back at the starting point. If this is all the knot that you wish, you will still have to bury the ends. Remember that anytime you finish a knot or any braiding, it is best to go under at least three times and not rely on an under one or under two to hold the end. Never cut off extra ends until the knot is finished. (By "finished," we mean that you have done all the interweaves desired, gone back and tightened the knot if needed, and rolled the knot on a smooth surface to make sure it is smooth and even. See chapter 14.) To prepare for the following interweave, make sure the knot is spaced to allow room for the interweave. An awl or other pointed tool is required to help do these steps.

Below is a review of the steps noted above. We will later make some changes to standardize them further for our summary Key to Knots.

1. Make clockwise pass	01
2. O1	U1,01
3. U1, O1	O1, U1, O1
4. O1, U1, O1	U1, O1, U1, O1
5. U1, O1, U1, O1	O1, U1, O1, U1, O1
6. O1, U1, O1, U1, O1	U1, O1, U1, O1, U1, O1

If you look at this written pattern, you will start to see some patterns in addition to the one noted earlier. For example, the last entry of any pass is over one. If you read the columns from top to bottom, they all alternate over, under. On another page you will find where this formula has been continued to eight bights. The patterns in these instructions will allow you to expand the instructions to an infinite number of bights. In reality, four, six, and eight bights should be enough to know for most rawhide work. The knots will be expanded by the use of interweaves rather than an increased number of bights in the foundation knot. The four, six, or eight bight foundation knot instructions can be used to tie an eight, twelve, or sixteen bight foundation by simply doing each step twice. In other words, the look of step 1 would change from a "U" to a "UU". Then each numbered section will follow and repeat before going to the next numbered section.

Your most likely errors will originate from forgetting the cautions noted earlier in the third and fifth passes. (In later notations we will use a + at these points to remind you of the repeated step.) Note that there is a similar repetition on the end of one, three, and five. These we will not mark in any special notation because all the lines end in over. It just is not as likely a spot to cause error. If you are tying a knot and forget where you are, knowing that the end of any pass will be an over should allow you to finish the foundation knot.

With the interweave, you can introduce a new lace or continue. (If you started with a long enough piece, then you can continue. If you started with a short piece, then a new strand can be worked in here. If color is to be added, then this is the time and place to start.) If the original lace is not to continue, then you should work onto the original dead end or number one. Then back the original dead end out enough to free it of an over. Slip it back in the original direction and you should have a smoother transition. Do not cut anything shorter at this time as you will have to use these ends later when tightening. In some of the photographs, I have hidden the foundation's working end under the dead end and the rest of the knot. The dead end has been left exposed for reference. If the interweave is a different color, then you will be developing some bands of color or rings of interweave in the knot. These bands or rings I am referring to make V-shaped or chevron patterns around the knot. These are within latitudes and thus I call them rings even though they are not straight.

If you continue with the original lace, then you are actually creating a minor flaw in the mathematics or symmetry of the knot. We will continue the knot in the following way:

7. O1, U1, O1, U2X   O1, U1, O1, U2X

The notation U2X means that you go under the adjacent two that form a cross or X. In the next steps we will also have to go under the interweave itself. Thus the instructions become under two that cross and one more. This one more is the interweave, and so you should be looking for the lace that is making a bight inside the knot and directly adjacent to the 2X. To save space we shall call this step U3X. The remaining instructions are:

8. O1, U1, O1, U3X	O1, U1, O1, U3X
9. O1, U1, O1, U3X	O2, U1, O1, U3X
10. O2, U1, O1, U3X	O2, U2, O1, U3X
11. O2, U2, O2, U3X	O2, U2, O2, U3X
12. O2, U2, O2, U3X	O2, U2, O2, *Under* to exit the knot

When you start to look at this section for patterns, you should notice that all of the columns are the over, under, over, under type. The change is the introduction of the 02 and U2 as you encounter the previous part of the interweave. On another page, this pattern has been extended for an eight-bight knot. Before you are done with the knot, you will have to go back and tighten it. When using an awl or other pointed instrument, it is probably best not to have a sharp point, as that can scratch or cut your work. Work the point under an over pass and lift up. The slack thus collected will then be moved to the next spot, where you repeat this process, over and over again. Start your tightening where we ended the instructions. Work backwards through the knot by just following the string's progress. If you were too loose in your work, you may have to repeat the entire process. Once the knot is tight, the ends must be buried as described before. Then the entire knot can be rolled on a hard, clean surface. You can use your hand or another object on top to apply pressure and help in the rolling process.

This ends the instructions for the small round button. To help in the later descriptions we shall call this knot the "Six Bight of 1X in the Formula." This is shortened to "6B, X = 1." (The term Turk's Head is used so often in connection with so many knots that I have chosen not to use it in this work.) The mathematical description by number of bights is more useful when trying to "look up" or describe most of these knots. We will now present a short summary of this knot. Then we will present the formula for a longer form (X = 2). Finally the Key to Knots formula will be presented. This is actually X = 3, but can be expanded to any length. Now for a summary of 6B, X = 1.

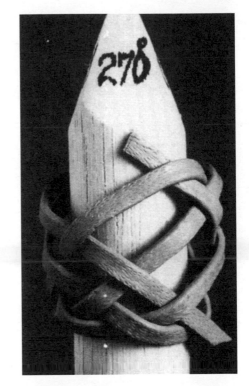

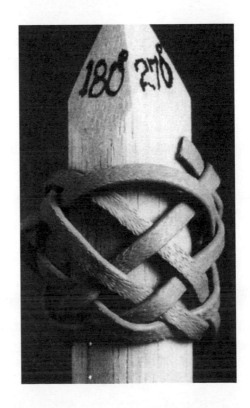

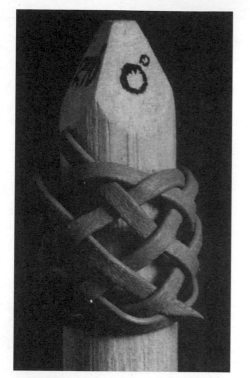

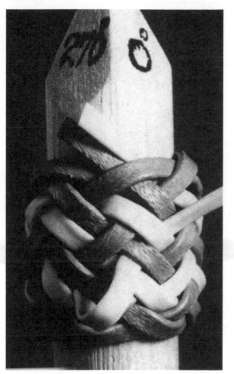

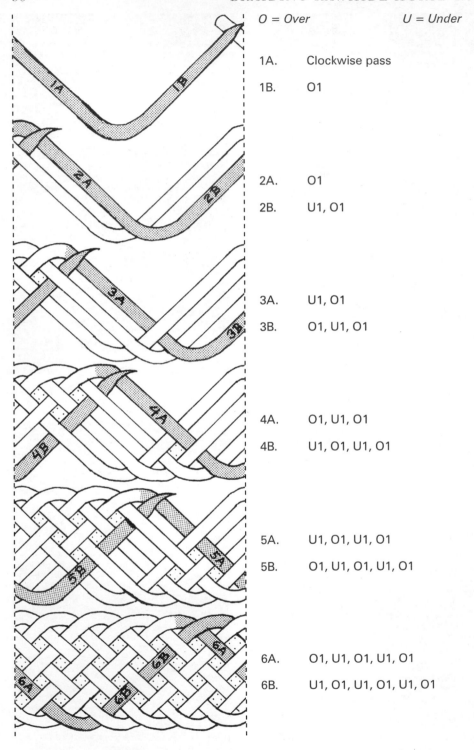

O = Over   U = Under

1A.	Clockwise pass
1B.	O1
2A.	O1
2B.	U1, O1
3A.	U1, O1
3B.	O1, U1, O1
4A.	O1, U1, O1
4B.	U1, O1, U1, O1
5A.	U1, O1, U1, O1
5B.	O1, U1, O1, U1, O1
6A.	O1, U1, O1, U1, O1
6B.	U1, O1, U1, O1, U1, O1

Fig. 25. Six-bight small round knot (6B, X = 1), steps 1A through 6B.

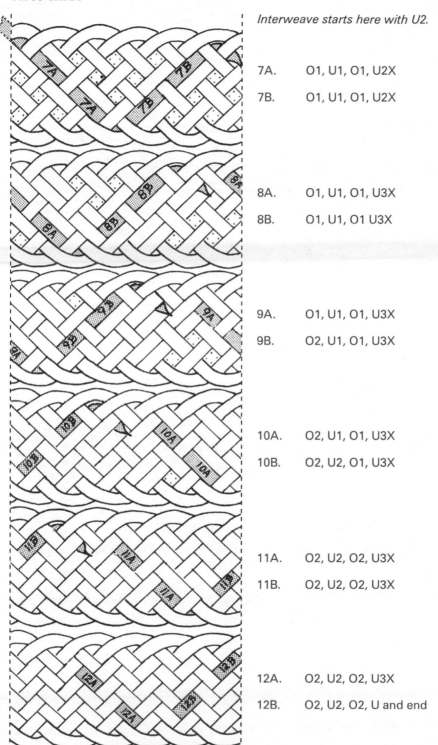

Interweave starts here with U2.

7A.	O1, U1, O1, U2X
7B.	O1, U1, O1, U2X
8A.	O1, U1, O1, U3X
8B.	O1, U1, O1 U3X
9A.	O1, U1, O1, U3X
9B.	O2, U1, O1, U3X
10A.	O2, U1, O1, U3X
10B.	O2, U2, O1, U3X
11A.	O2, U2, O2, U3X
11B.	O2, U2, O2, U3X
12A.	O2, U2, O2, U3X
12B.	O2, U2, O2, U and end

Fig. 26. Six-bight small round knot (6B, X = 1), steps 7A through 12B.

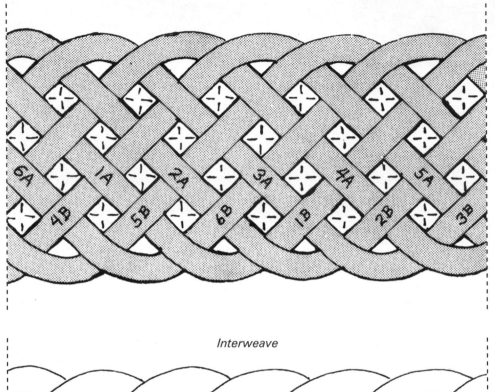

Interweave

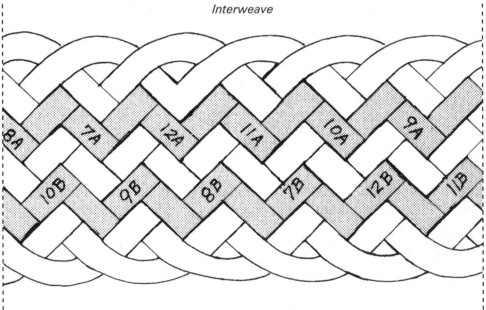

Fig. 27. Finished six-bight knot (6B, X = 1), all steps numbered.

1.A. Make clockwise pass
  B. O1

2.A. O1
  B. U1, O1

3.A. U1, O1 +
  B. O1, U1, O1

4.A. O1, U1, O1
  B. U1, O1, 111, O1

5.A. U1, O1, U1, O1 +
  B. O1, U1, O1, U1, O1

6.A. O1, U1, O1, U1, O1
  B. U1, O1, U1, O1, 111, O1

Interweave starts here with U2.

7.A. O1, U1, O1, U2X
  B. O1, U1, O1, U2X

8.A. O1, 111, O1, U3X
  B. O1, U1, O1, U3X

9.A. O1, U1, O1, U3X
  B. O2, U1, O1, U3X

10.A. O2, U1, O1, U3X
  B. O2, U2, O1, U3X

11.A. O2, U2, O1, U3X
  B. O2, U2, O2, U3X

12.A. O2, U2, O2, U3X
  B. O2, U2, O2, Under & bury ends

Fig. 28. Six-bight small round knot with two rings of interweave (6B, X = 1). Each numbered line represents the path of the string for one complete cycle of the knot.

Foundation

Fig. 29. Six-bight long knot foundation (6B, X = 2).

Fig. 30. Completed six-bight long knot with interweave (6B, X= 2).

1.A. Make clockwise pass (bight same side as start)
  B. Over the first pass two times (X = 2)

2.A. O1   +O1
  B. U1, O1   U1, O1

3.A. U1, O1   U1, O1
  B. O1, U1, O1   +O1, U1, O1

4.A. O1, U1, O1   +O1, U1, O1
  B. U1, O1, U1, O1   U1, O1, U1, O1

5.A. U1, O1, U1, O1   U1, O1, U1, O1
  B. O1, U1, O1, U1, O1 +O1, U1, O1, U1, O1

6.A. O1, U1, O1, U1, O1 +O1, U1, O1, U1, O1
  B. U1, O1, U1, O1, U1, O1 U1, O1, U1, O1, U1, O1

Interweave starts here with U2.

7.A. O1, U1, O1, U1, O1, U1, O1, U1, O1, U2X
  B. O1, U1, O1, U1, O2, U1, O1, U1, O1, U2X

8.A. O1, U1, O1, U1, O2, U1, O1, U1, O1, U3X
  B. O1, U1, O1, U1, O2, U2, O1, U1, O1, U3X

9.A. O1, U1, O1, U1, O2, U2, O1, U1, O1, U3X
  B. O2, U1, O1, U1, O2, U2, O2, U1, O1, U3X

10.A. O2, U1, O1, U1, O2, U2, O2, U1, O1, U3X
  B. O2, U2, O1, U1, O2, U2, O2, U2, O1, U3X

11.A. O2, U2, O1, U1, O2, U2, O2, U2, O1, U3X
  B. O2, U2, O2, U1, O2, U2, O2, U2, O2, U3X

12.A. O2, U2, O2, U1, O2, U2, O2, U2, O2, U3X
  B. O2, U2, O2, U2, O2, U2, O2, U2, O2, U to end

Fig. 31. Six-bight long knot with five rings of interweave (6B, X = 2). Note: The + is used to draw attention to the repeat of an "over," which quite often is the cause of easily-made mistakes.

Fig. 32. Six-bight long knot foundation (6B, X = 3).

Fig. 33. Six-bight knot (6B, X = any number).

1.	A.	Wrap clockwise.		
	B.	Return back going over ..X.. number of times.		
2.	A.	Over	..X.. times	
	B.	U1, O1	..X.. times	
3.	A.	U1, O1	..X.. times	
	B.	O1, 111, O1	+	..X.. times
4.	A.	O1, U1, O1	+	..X.. times
	B.	U1, O1, 111, O1	..X.. times	
5.	A.	U1, O1, U1, O1	..X.. times	
	B.	O1, U1, O1, U1, O1 +	..X.. times	
6.	A.	O1, U1, O1, U1, O1 +	..X.. times	
	B.	U1, O1, U1, O1, U101	..X.. times	

For six-bight, the interweave starts here with U2.

Start at the left of the instruction line and follow the instructions as far as possible. That portion between parentheses is the pattern to be repeated as needed. When you run out of room to continue a pattern, the last under will have to be upgraded to the last entry on the line of instructions.

7.	A.	O1, U1, O1, U1, (O1, U1, O1, U1, O1, U1) O1, U1, O1, U1, O1, U2X
	B.	O1, U1, O1, U1, (O2, U1, O1, U1, O1, U1) O2, U1, O1, U1, O1, U2X
8.	A.	O1, U1, O1, U1, O2, (U1, O1, U1, O1, U1, O2) U1, O1, U1, O1, U3X
	B.	O1, U1, O1, U1, O2, (U2, O1, U1, O1, U1, O2) U2, O1, U1, O1, U3X
9.	A.	(O1, U1, O1, U1, O2, U2) O1, U1, 01, U3X
	B.	(O2, U1, O1, U1, O2, U2) O2, U1, O1, U3X
10.	A.	O2, (U1, O1,U1, O2, U2, O2) U1, O1, U3X
	B.	O2, (U2, O1, U1, O2, U2, O2) U2, 01, U3X
11.	A.	O2, U2, (O1, U1, O2, U2, O2, U2) O1, U3X
	B.	O2, U2, (O2, U1, O2, U2, O2, U2) O2, U3X
12.	A.	O2, U2, O2, (U1, O2, U2, O2, U2, O2) U3X
	B.	O2, U2, O2, (U2, O2, U2, O2, U2, O2) End under.

Fig. 34. Key to Knots—six-bight of any length (6B, X = any number).

Fig. 35. The foundation knot for six-bight, X = 3.

Fig. 36. The finished six-bight knots demonstrating (left to right) X = 1, X = 2, and X = 3.

1. Make clockwise pass	O		
2. O	U, O		
3. U, O	O, U, O		
4. O, U, O	U, O, U, O		
5. U, O, U, O	O, U, O, U, O		
6. O, U, O, U, O	U, O, U, O, U, O		
7. U, O, U, O, U, O	O, U, O, U, O, U, O		
8. O, U, O, U, O, U, O	U, O, U, O, U, O, U, O		

Interweave start U2

9. O1, U1, O1, U1, O1,	U2X	O1, U1, O1, U1, O1, U2X	
10. O1, U1, O1, U1, 01,	U3X	O1, U1, O1, U1, O1, U3X	
11. O1, U1, O1, U1, O1,	U3X	O2, U1, O1, U1, O1, U3X	
12. O2, U1, O1, U1, O1,	U3X	O2, U2, O1, U1, O1, U3X	
13. O2, U2, O1, U1, O1,	U3X	O2, U2, O2, U1, O1, U3X	
14. O2, U2, O2, U1, O1,	U3X	O2, U2, O2, U2, O1, U3X	
15. O2, U2, O2, U2, O1,	U3X	O2, U2, O2, U2, O2, U3X	
16. O2, U2, O2, U2, O2,	U3X	O2, U2, O2, U2, O2, U3X	

Fig. 37. The formula continued to eight bights with three rings of interweave (8B X= 1).

I gave this knot the nickname "W Round Button" because the long- short-short-long pattern looks like a W. In the photographs you will see this knot used on reins and the large knot on the hobbles. I have also seen it used flat around the leather stinger or double fall of a quirt. There are several features about this knot that make it very nice: it has a nice simple pattern that shows off very well; and the bights are not sharp and thus make a strong, smooth knot. This is a good example of a knot that can be tied tight from the start.

Instructions are presented in a format like the earlier examples. This knot requires about 3 feet of lace.

1.A. One wrap clockwise.
  B. Return to make a bight just before you get to the start.
2.A. Parallel to and tight against the original (1A).
  B. O1
3.A. O1
  B. O2
4.A. O2
  B. O3
5.A. O3
  B. O3, U1
6.A. O3, U1
  B. O3, U2
7.A. O3, U2
  B. O3, U2, O1
8.A. O3, U2, O1
  B. O3, U2, O2
9.A. O3, U2, O2
  B. O3, U2, O2, U1
10.A. O3, U2, O2, U1
  B. O3, U2, O2, U2
11.A. O3, U2, O2, U2
  B. O3, U2, O2, U3
12.A. O3, U2, O2, U3
  B. O3, U2, O2, U3

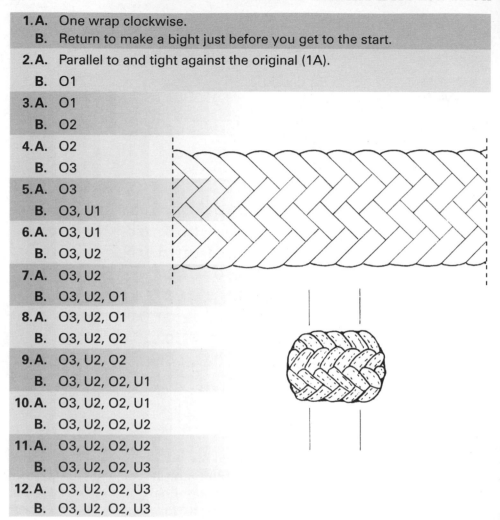

Fig. 38. Twelve-bight with a 3-2-2-3 pattern (the W round button).

There are several ways to end this knot. Probably the easiest is to put your needle on what was the dead end and go under three just beside what served as the working end (12B). Pull tight on these two ends which are going in opposite directions. Then cut both as close to the knot as possible.

Fig. 39. The 3-2-2-3 or W knot compared to the 6B, X = 1.
These are on reins made by Jack Shepard.

6. FOUR PATTERNS OF INTERWEAVES

This section is based on some letters written by the late Ernie Ladouceur. Here is a most interesting excerpt from one (June 15,1964).

> I never tried to learn to tie buttons from a book and never found it too easy to do so. . . .We will make it merely a matter of memory and practice and not of problems.
>
> For instance, when you try to learn to tie a button from a book, you never see all of the button at one time. You only see the one third that is facing you. You then have the problem of learning the continuity of the button so you can memorize the important points. The outcome is that solving the problem of the continuity of the button was a much harder job than remembering it after the problem was solved.... I have noticed that people when learning to weave a button, try to remember that they went over two and under one or some such thing in a certain part of a certain button.... A better way is to remember the continuity of the button and how it compares or differs from another button. Continuity seems to be the word that is the most applicable to the problem.

We have already introduced the idea of the clockwise wrap followed by the crossing of the dead end. Each time it crosses, I have counted this as X. The total number of X's has been shown as X = 1, X = 2, X = 3, etc. Ernie called this a "one, two, or three turn button." We continue our quote from the same letter:

> Years ago I found the interweaving of a framework very confusing, especially when using a colored string or when weaving O-U-3 or more or possibly O-U-3 in part of a button and then adding O-U-4 or more in certain parts. After we developed our present system of interweaving, we

do not have any difficulty in interweaving as we may want. [This is] because we know that there are four simple interweaves that do not change with any number of bights, or any lengths, or with odd or even number of bights. It is only the framework that changes for each different button. Being that the framework is always only O-U-1, it in turn is quite easy to learn in its many forms.

In comparing the interweaves you will find the #1 form and the #2 forms are similar because they both start the same and finish the same. Also, that the #3 form and the #4 form are similar because they both start the same and finish the same. You will also find that if you had learned the #2 form first, that you would have no trouble learning the #3 form as they are the same except reversed. At the same time you would have learned that the #2 and #3 forms are the same as one half of the #1 and #4 forms. The fact is that when the important points are brought to your attention, none are difficult to learn and after one form is learned, the rest are much simplified.

After the proper framework is made, you need the answers to a number of key questions:

1. How do you come back into the framework to
   start the interweave in relation to the dead end?
2. How do you tuck up in relation to the
   string to the right or left of the deadend?
3. On reaching the top of the framework, do you stay
   inside the framework to turn down, or outside, or even
   with it in relation to the bight at the top of the framework?
4. How do you tuck down in relation to the string
   making the bight at the top of the framework?
5. How do you split pairs and how do you turn up after reaching
   the bight at the bottom in relation to the bight at the bottom?

The four types of interweaves are numbered as follows:

Type 1: Inside top and bottom
Type 2: Outside on bottom
Type 3: Outside on top
Type 4: Outside top and bottom

You should recognize that all the instructions up to this point have given you the Type 1 variation of interweave. We will present the other variations in the form of drawings. The drawings are all based on a four-bight knot, which can also be described as a four-bight, five-part knot. The term "five-part" is best explained by counting the number of strands cut when the knot is opened out as shown in the drawings. I have not used this term in other places as it might be confusing.

To tie or weave a button that has a good appearance, it should be tight and straight. In order to be straight when finished, the framework should be straight before the interweave is begun. In order to be straight, all the crosses in the weave should be in line and this line should come out in the middle of a bight at one end of the button and between two bights at the other end. After you have woven a framework and before starting the interweave, always sight down the row of crosses and make sure all crosses are in line as mentioned above. After a while the framework will always be straight and this will not be any problem. ... If you find that you have woven a button with some spiral to it, the best advice I can give you is to take a sharp knife, cut it off of the core, and weave another button. It won't take much of this before you will find you seldom weave a button that isn't straight.

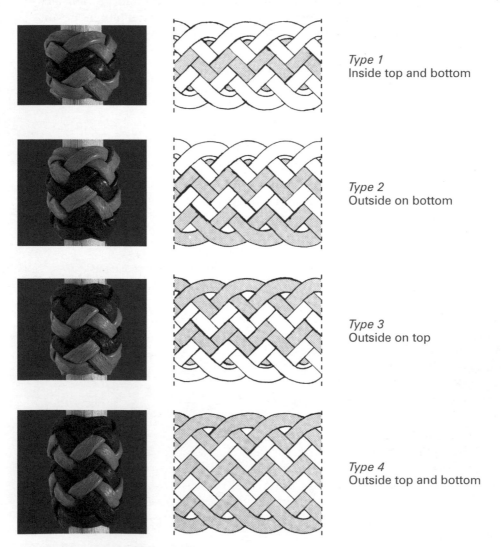

Type 1
Inside top and bottom

Type 2
Outside on bottom

Type 3
Outside on top

Type 4
Outside top and bottom

Fig. 40. Four types of interweave.

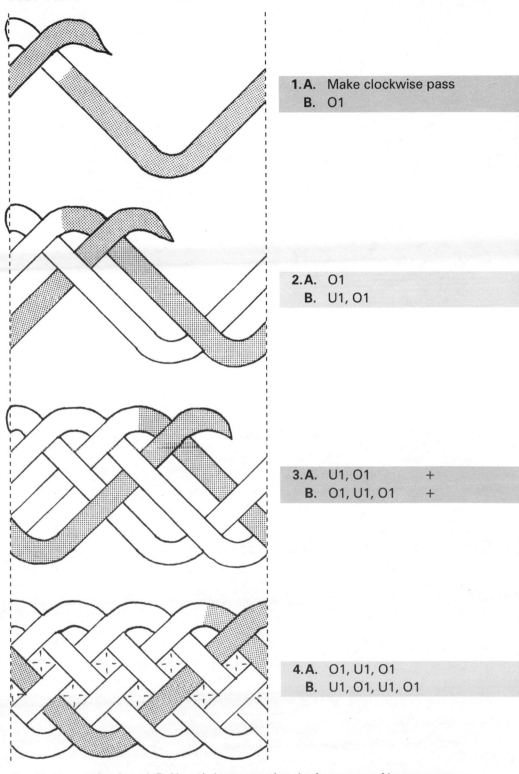

1.A. Make clockwise pass
  B. O1

2.A. O1
  B. U1, O1

3.A. U1, O1   +
  B. O1, U1, O1   +

4.A. O1, U1, O1
  B. U1, O1, U1, O1

Fig. 41. Foundation knot (4B, X = 1) demonstrating the four types of interweave.

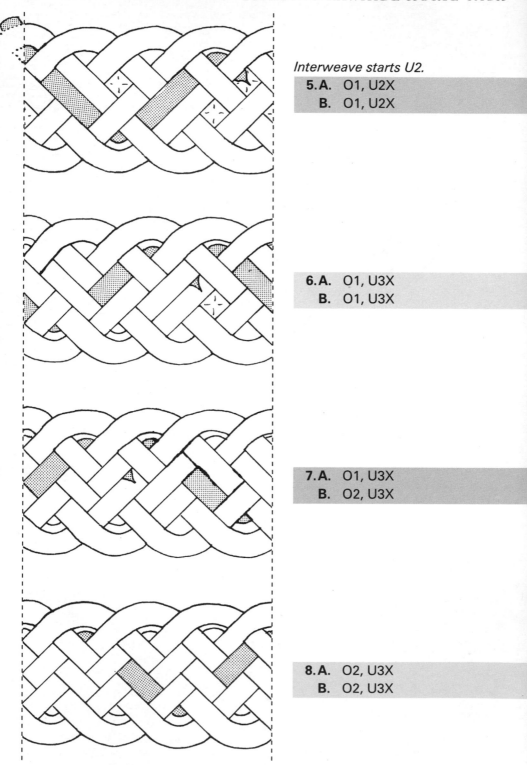

Interweave starts U2.

5.A. O1, U2X
  B. O1, U2X

6.A. O1, U3X
  B. O1, U3X

7.A. O1, U3X
  B. O2, U3X

8.A. O2, U3X
  B. O2, U3X

Fig. 42. Type 1 interweave, inside top and bottom.

Interweave starts U2.

5.A. O1, U1, O1
   B. O1, U1, O2, U2X

6.A. O1, U1, O2
   B. O1, U2, O2, U2X

7.A. O1, U2, O2
   B. O2, U2, O2, U2X

8.A. O2, U2, O2
   B. U1, O2, U2, O2, U & end

Fig. 43. Type 2 interweave, outside on bottom.

Interweave starts U2.

5. A. O1, U2X
   B. O1, U1, O2

6. A. O1, U1, O2, U2X
   B. O1, U2, O2

7. A. O1, U2, O2, U2X
   B. O2, U2, O2

8. A. O2, U2, O2, U3X
   B. O2, U2, O2, U & end

Fig. 44. Type 3 interweave, outside on top.

5. A. O1, U1, O1, U1, O1
**   B.** O1, U1, O2, U1, O1

6. A. O1, U1, O2, U1, O1
**   B.** U1, O1, U1, O2, U2, O1

7. A. U1, O1, U1, O2, U2, O1
**   B.** U1, O2, U1, O2, U2, O2

8. A. U1, O2, U1, O2, U2, O2
**   B.** U1, O2, U2, O2, U2, O2 & end

Fig. 45. Type 4 interweave, outside top and bottom.

As you add your interweave into the framework, you will notice that the knot becomes tighter. "Experience will tell you how tight to weave the framework in order to have a really tightly woven finished button." Ernie explains that:

> Up to this point, you should be able to weave any framework with an even number of bights and any whole number of turns of the core. These frameworks can all be interwoven in the four different forms as the sketches show. It is impossible to weave a framework with one string in which the number of bights and the number of parts has a common divisor.

For the purposes of this book, we will not get into examples of exceptions to this rule. As we stated earlier, because there are still braiders in this and other countries who are trying to make a living at rawhide braiding, we will not be going into fancy or collector types of braiding. However, these drawings should give the reader some very good ideas on possible variations. The facts are that with the instructions already given, you can make all but one of the knots needed for the horse tack that we will be discussing. That one remaining knot will be presented in Chapter 8.

You can also tie buttons that are a fraction of a turn, and you can work in fractions above one turn. "The same may be said about frameworks with various number of bights, but they are not a full turn of the core.

"After you have made the four-bight, five-part framework and have interwoven them in the four different forms, you will want to interweave different frameworks." Following is a suggested way that you can use to develop different frameworks.

Take the instructions for the Type 1 interweave and write down the instruction that this string makes in relation to itself. The result is as follows:

1.A.	Down.	
B.	Make the bight short of the start.	
2.A.	Parallel to the first.	
B.	U1	
3.A.	U1	
B.	U1, O1	
4.A.	U1, O1	
B.	U1, O1	

This gives us a four-bight, three-part framework. Ernie Ladouceur said, "This new framework is a fraction of one turn and you can see that it differs greatly from any full turn framework. This new framework does not look too promising, but this is what you can do with it."

Come back into the framework with the same lace. This will be short of the dead end (it does not cross the dead end).

5.A. U1, O1
  B. U2, O1
6.A. U2, O1
  B. U2, O2 splitting pairs
7.A. U2, O2 splitting pairs
  B. U2, O2 splitting pairs

You now have a "nice woven ring knot." This knot can be easily expanded to an over-three, under-three pattern.

The four-bight, three-part framework (from above) "can also be expanded into a 7 bight, three part framework." To do this, start by "tucking the working end parallel to the dead end. [Pull] them away from each other to make more space between them.... Then bring the top string over the lower string in that space." Then weave the working end under one and over one to make the longer framework. This framework can also be woven into an over two, under two ring knot. "It can be woven in #2, #3, or #4 forms and can be woven into over, under three or more in all forms. [It can also be] interwoven in the Gaucho or cross stitch weave.... The base of all of this and very much more are the four interweaves."

In conclusion, here are a few suggestions. When weaving any straight button, "a better job can be done by weaving in the #4 form.... The button can be woven tighter and more easily in this form. In weaving any round or irregular shaped button, the other three forms are preferred as the interweave can be made to suit the occasion." A combination of all can be used for the over-three and under-three, patterns of larger numbers, or where using colors.

7. COMBINING INTERWEAVES

There are many possible combinations of the four basic types of interweaves. They can be enlarged to over and under patterns of three, four, five, six, or more. For demonstration we will use the Type 4 for a start and then add a Type 3. The instructions below start at the point after you have tied the Type 4 pattern as shown earlier in Figs. 41 and 45. To make the additional interweave, you will have to add to the formula originally presented. In the following instructions we will still use the U3X instructions even though we will not be directly below the cross. If you wish, you can think of the U1 at the end of the A. pass and the U2 at the start of the B. pass as combining to form a U3X. As you work, you can use the previously tied parts of the knot to guide you in the pattern.

This is only one example of many possible combinations. You will want to try your hand at other patterns. If you have trouble with a pattern, you may wish to try the following crutch. Tie the foundation and first interweave. Then work in some short, colored scraps to develop the pattern the way you wish. Once you have this completed with the short strings, take a long string and follow the short string's path with the new string. Remove one step (for instance, an under three), and replace it with the longer string. Once you have done this for the entire knot, you can write down your formula in reverse as you withdraw the string one step at a time.

It is important to remember that the previous examples have been presented to teach principles. They have to be adaped to the particular knot being tied. Here is one example of combining interweaves (4 B, X = 1, Type 4 then Type 3):

9.	A.	O2, U2, O2, U2, O2, U2X
	B.	O2, U2, O3, U2, O2
10.	A.	O2, U2, O3, U2, O2, U3X
	B.	O2, U2, O3, U3, O2
11.	A.	U1, O2, U2, O3, U3, O2, U3X
	B.	O3, U2, O3, U3, O2
12.	A.	U1, O3, U2, O3, U3, O3, U3X
	B.	O3, U3, O3, U3, O3, and end

Fig. 46. Example of over three, under three.

8. KNOTS USING MULTIPLE STRANDS

In this chapter we will be presenting two basic patterns of knots that can be made to any desired length. These patterns can also be mixed in the same knot to make some interesting designs. (This is the technique that many of the old-time braiders used for all their knots, because there are only a few steps for one to remember.) The main disadvantage of the method is that there are a lot of ends to bury. Thus it is mostly used for longer knots, such as the one that is used on reins to cover the end "turn back" and splice. In this book we will talk about the technique in relation to the long nose knot on the bosal.

So far, almost all of the knots have had the V patterns pointing in the same direction as the long axis of the knot. This is usually referred to as the herringbone pattern. In the 3-2-2-3 knot (or W knot) the pattern points around the knot. In the following instructions we demonstrate an over two, under two pattern that also goes around the knot. This is commonly called the gaucho pattern. Gail Hought, of McKinleyville, California, says, "The gaucho weave usually turns nicer on the ends, especially when using larger strings." In other words, the gaucho pattern will hold better to the core ring knot and make a smoother end to your knot.

We have presented the following instructions so that the resulting knots will be the same as those in the photographs. These instructions can be viewed in a mirror to obtain the mirror image patterns. In fact, if you turn to the final drawing and turn it upside down you will see that the herringbone pattern is the same as in the earlier drawings. You might say that we are showing the "B. bight" end of the knot. As a result of this reversal, some of the drawings show the working end going from lower right to upper left. When you get to the wraps of the strings over the core, they are still clockwise, though you might say that the wraps go from "B." to "A." if you wish to compare to the earlier knots.

There are two patterns, herringbone and gaucho, and combinations of both. In the drawings we will use gaucho on the ends and then change to herringbone. In one of the photographs, this is done in reverse, with gaucho in the center of the knot. In other examples, only the herringbone is used. (In another piece, not shown, the patterns change from one to the other many times throughout the knot.)

Now let's start our instructions. In the drawings we have shown six strands, but this technique can be used for any number of strings. Some of the larger bosals that are shown in the photographs probably used eight or nine strands. Depending on the size of the work and the size of your strings, only some trial and error on your part can tell you exactly how many to use. While following the first five drawings, you will be working on a flat surface. When I was first shown this technique, the braider did these steps in his lap. Actually the work area is the top of your leg, between the knee and the hip. In the drawings, there will be mention of "short" and "long." By this we will mean the short end of the string and the long end of the string, based on the location of the starting points. It is suggested that you make the long ends twice the length of the short ends.

1. Place one string on your leg as shown, short end to the top (or right) and long end to the bottom (or left).
2. Place a second string across the first. The short end is to the top (left this time) and the long end is to the bottom (or right).
3. Place a third string over the second and parallel to the first.
4. Make a bight in the first string to bring it over the third string as shown.
5. Continue this pattern until all the strings are started in an over one, under one pattern with a space of one string's width between each strand.

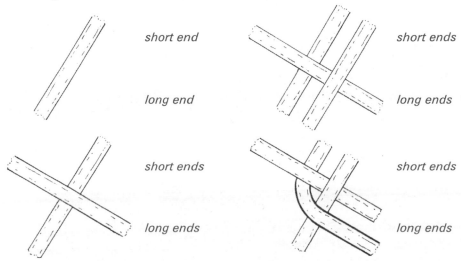

Fig. 47. Multiple strands, steps 1 to 4.

6. Bend this work around the core or work to be covered. Make a bight
    in string number two. Then make a bight in the last string started
    and bring it over the number two string. Continue on with under
    one, over one for a short distance. Do the same for any of the others
    that need to be extended for any distance.

long ends   *short ends*

Fig. 48. Multiple strands, step 6.

7. Tie some twine around this part of the work to hold it in place. Then
    separate the short strands to the right and the long strands to the left.
8. Wrap the short strands in a clockwise wrap past the desired length of
    the finished knot. These should be parallel to each other and spaced
    apart the width of one strand. These wraps should be extended well
    past the ring knot or desired length. The extra is thus kept out of the
    way. Take some twine and tie the short strands down so the ends will
    not get in your way. You will not be working with these short ends
    for a while.
9. Work each strand down in an over one, under one pattern for the
    desired length.

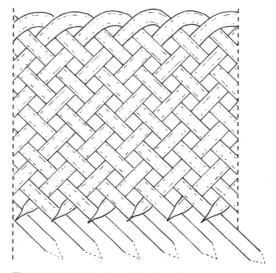

Fig. 49. Multiple strands, step 9.

10. When you are ready to make a bight and go back up, make sure that each long strand is at the same distance and has ended with an over (over the short). Each long strand will then go under the adjacent long strand as shown in the drawing.

11. This is still an over one, under one pattern. You are now making a pair with the adjacent short. Take all of the longs to the top of the knot.

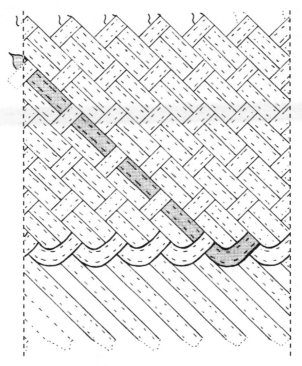

Fig. 50. Multiple strands, steps 10 and 11.

12. At this point half of the ends are at the top of the knot (the long strands) and the other half are at the bottom. Those at the bottom have been called the "short" strands to this point. If you check, these lengths may now be the same as, or longer than, the others. In reality, it no longer matters which end is "top" or "bottom," nor does it matter which end has "short" or "long" strings. You will be doing exactly the same to both ends. Turn your work and check—both ends should look the same. Turn the drawing for step 11 upside down and you will see where you are right now in the instructions. Each end comes out from under a bight. Thus, make a bight and go over the adjacent strand that makes a bight. For the gaucho pattern that is being demonstrated, this will actually be over two, under two, over two, under two. Do this for all the strands at both ends. This pattern can be continued for the full length if you wish, but we will now demonstrate a change to the herringbone pattern.

13. The transition must be made after an under two part of the sequence. The change consists of over one, under one. Then you are ready to continue with the over two, under two pattern for the remainder of the knot.

14. There are two ways to finish this knot. The ends can be staggered for the length of the knot so that they are in a straight line. Then the ends can be buried under three or more. When the bosal is curved, this straight line should then be on the inside. In the photographs there is another ending shown—the ends are brought out next to the over one transition point. Then the end is cut off flush with the work. Thus the ends are staggered around the work at a point where it is not obvious. In fact it makes the over one look like the other over two parts of the weave. Here you need to decide where or how you wish to stagger and bury the ends.

Gaucho

Herringbone

Fig. 51. Multiple strands, final steps.

You should by now have noticed that both the gaucho and herringbone patterns have this final pass splitting the pairs that were created in step 11. The photographs show this pattern being used in rawhide bosal nose buttons.

9. OTHER KNOTS

Although this book is not intended to cover all knots, a couple of books that just about accomplish that feat need to be mentioned.

The first was published in 1939 and its 690 pages make up the very interesting *Encyclopedia of Knots and Fancy Rope Work* by Raoul Graumont and John Hensel. In it, plaiting is referred to as "sennit braiding." Most of the knots that we have been talking about are covered in a chapter on "Turk's Heads."

Another book worth having is the 528-page *Encyclopedia of Rawhide and Leather Braiding* by Bruce Grant, published in 1972. Because Grant's books have been the standard for many years on this subject, several of his names and terms are now accepted by many braiders. Both of these books are still in print and are listed with other references in the "Recommended Reading" section at the back of this book.

A knot that is seen in many of our photographs is named by Grant as "The Spanish Ring Knot." We have already presented one explanation of a ring knot. It is pictured on Plate 161 of Grant's *Encyclopedia*. This knot is easy to learn and fast to do. The easiest way that I have found to explain this knot is to have someone braid three-plait using three strings. This is shown in our table of plaits, Fig. 15. Start with one string around your dowel. Cross at the start with an over. Then go around and cross the second near the dead end and then under the dead end. Now comes the trick — the first pass (dead end) and the second are both going around the core parallel to each other. Take the first pass and tuck it under the second pass. This gives you some new bights. Then continue your working end under one and over one. You should be able to see that this pattern looks like the three-plait braid. It can be continued as needed or enlarged with interweaves.

Another knot is the covering knot for the hobbles center ring. For this you are directed to Plate 52, Figs. 1 through 7, in Grant's *Encyclopedia* (see Appendix). This knot is easy to do and makes a very nice cover over the metal ring. It helps finish off the hobbles and separates the homemade (or pride in workmanship) from the store bought.

Plate 76, "How to Make the Tamale," is valuable. Also, Plate 78 on "How to Make a San Juan Honda" is worth studying.

The list could go on, but by now you are anxious to start an actual item. We will now present ideas and instructions for reatas, hobbles, reins, and bosals. There are many other items that one could make, but this will cover the items that most people will be interested in making.

10. THE REATA

There are a few cowboys and buckaroos who still prefer to use rawhide ropes. La reata is the original Mexican phrase that became the modem English term "lariat." All of the basics on rawhide preparation have been greatly influenced by braiders who made reatas for everyday use. This chapter has been greatly influenced by the ideas of one braider, Bill Dor- rance of Salinas, California. It wets 1931 when Bill came to California and started making and using rawhide reatas; so, as this is being written [in 1983], he's been rawhiding for more than fifty years. Asked why he still uses rawhide reatas, Bill responded, "They have more life, and carry out better."

Bill has made reatas that were over 90 feet long, but he says that he usually starts with a reata of about 65 feet. By the time the reata is worn out, it has gradually been shortened to about 45 to 50 feet. Any reata that is shorter than 40 feet is only good for working in a corral on foot. "Show" reatas that measure 10 or 15 feet are of no use. One day Bill held one of his average lariats for me to measure. The circumference of the loop was 15 feet and, further, he held several small coils in his throwing hand, a length between his hands, and the remaining coils in his other hand. He pointed out that sometimes, in his earlier years, he had to make 35- to 48-foot throws. Obviously, a 10- to 15-foot lariat is not worth having on the saddle.

One of the first things that I did with rawhide was to splice a number of reatas that had been shortened for show tack. The owners had changed their minds and no longer wished them short. The shortest that I would ever shorten a reata to is 40 feet. With a very tight 10-inch diameter coil, it sticks out less than 2 inches from the saddle.

We measured Bill's reatas and found that 11/32 of an inch was about the standard diameter. The maximum was 3/8 inch, and 5/16 inch was the lightest. Bill explained that he didn't need a reata larger than 3/8 inch in diameter. He felt that the smaller diameter offered less air resistance when throwing, and was less bulky to handle. When made of good quality rawhide and used properly, his reatas were able to get the job done.

Some of Bill's reatas have a core. The core is a strip of rawhide that is about half the width of a regular string. It runs through the middle for the full length of the braiding. The advantage of a core is that it helps make the braiding smooth and round. Four- and six-plaits can be braided without a core. Eight-plaits will result in a square cross section unless a core is used. Everything larger than this will require a core. Another advantage of a core is in making repairs. If one plait of the reata gets broken or damaged (for instance, on a sharp rock), then you may wish to make a repair. Start by unbraiding the broken plait for about 1 foot in both directions. Then remove the core from that section and an additional five inches more in both directions. Cut the broken plait ends to 5-1/2 inches. Work the ends in to replace the core. Then braid in a new length with enough at each end to get buried under the good area where the extra 5 inches of core were removed. Once hammered and rolled, such a repair should be fairly smooth and hard to find.

In this book, we will be talking about braided, rather than twisted, rawhide. To braid a reata, you will need to start with four lengths of rawhide strings. These should be about 1/4 to 5/16 inch wide and about 90 feet long. You will leave 14 to 16 inches unbraided on the end to be used for attaching the honda. Bill leaves this length on both ends of his reatas. When one end gets worn, he can remove the honda from one end and put it on the other. For a first reata, you should probably not use a core. For later efforts, you may decide to use a core if you wish.

Place your strings in water for a short time. Then shake off the extra water and place the strings in moist sacks or rags until the moisture content is uniform and right. This is usually half an hour. Knowing when the rawhide is just right will be learned from experience. The most common error that most beginners make is to try to work with the strings too wet. Please remember that statement and do not get a bad habit started.

Braiding and rawhide can be hard on the hands. For protection, Bill uses leather pads on his hands. You can substitute old gloves with the fingers cut off. The string is wrapped once around the hand. As you pull on the string, one hand is braced behind the hip for more pulling power. At the same time the other hand will be pushing against the braid. Thus you will have both pulling and pushing power. This assures a good tight braid. It is also a good idea to have some kind of padding around your hips. Bill uses a couple of folded gunnysacks which are worn as aprons. The surface of these should be kept damp to help preserve the moisture of the rawhide. The rawhide should be kept moist during the braiding. Heavy soapsuds may be used on the section that is being worked. This seems to make the reata braid even tighter. Bill says that the actual braiding progresses at about 6 feet per hour. Starting with a cured hide, it will probably take over 30 hours before the reata is finished.

Once the reata length is braided, it should be hammered or rolled to make it smooth. Some prefer to pull the reata through a hole in a hardwood block. Shown in Fig. 52 is a tool for this purpose, made by Frank Hansen of

Lakeview, Oregon. (He also made the cutting tool pictured in Fig. 23.) The reata can then be stretched out straight and left to dry.

The next step is to make the honda. Bill Dorrance does not use the same style of San Juan honda that Bruce Grant described. Bill's hondas use a four and eight braid, and he prefers not to use the slit braid for the small eye of the honda. In Fig. 54 we show a honda by Ernie Ladouceur that does use the slit braid.

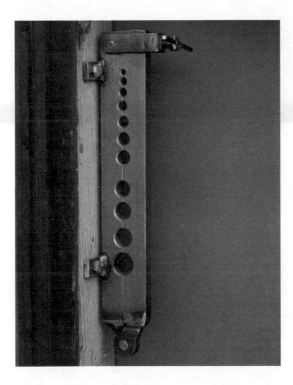

Fig. 52. This tool was made by Frank Hansen to help even round braids. The tool is opened, the item placed in the proper size hole, the tool is closed, and the full length of the plaiting is drawn through the hole.

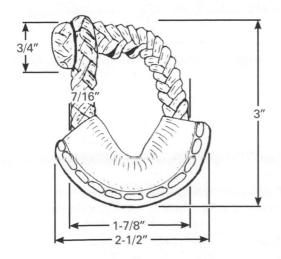

Fig. 53. A honda. The drawing is based on a honda that Bill Dorrance used until the reata "wore out." The differences between this and the San Juan honda have been noted in the text.

Fig. 54. A San Juan honda by the late Ernie Ladouceur. The braid back that secures the honda to the reata is by the author.

To make a honda, we will need four 1/4-inch strings about 36 inches long. Starting in the middle, braid four-plait for about five passes. Then bend the two ends together and see if it looks like a loop with a center opening of about 3/8 inch. If so, arrange the strings for an eight-plait braid. Place a 6-inch-long core into the braid. Braid eight-plait for the total length of the core and continue 1 /2 inch farther. Bend the length around and put the ends through the four-plait eye. This should be a snug fit for the 1/2-inch length without the core. Then the fit should be too tight to go further. The presence of the core should make this difference. Then take four outside strings and spread them out. They should be at 90-degree angles to each other. The center four plaits can be tied together if you wish. Take one string and bend it over to go 180 degrees opposite to where it was. Going around the core, do the same for the next string so that it crosses the first. Repeat for the third string. The fourth will go in the same direction, but will have to go under the first (through the bight of the first). This will give you a square pattern with each string forming an X with its neighbor. Now take a string and go under the loose neighbor and then up and under the above X. Do this for each string until all are in the center. Leave the excess lengths for now.

The next steps will require an old wooden hammer handle, which will have to be split lengthwise, or you can use two broom handles if you wish. You will also need one or two wooden wedges. Place the honda over the two parts of the wooden hammer handle. Then insert the wedges as needed to stretch the honda some. This will give the shape pictured in Fig. 55. Bill prefers an oblong shape rather than round. The oblong, in his opinion, holds its form better in wet weather, and "gives more freedom" to the reata when it is thrown.

This can be allowed to dry or you can go to the next step. Cut out a piece of rawhide for a burner or boot. Make sure it is moist and soft. Remove the wedges and position the burner rawhide where it should go. Bill places a second, short, narrow strip between the burner and the braiding to avoid frequently replacing the boot on the honda. Then reposition the wedges and tighten some. Now bend and shape the exposed burner rawhide to enclose the honda foundation. Once it is tight and shaped as you wish, poke holes for the desired stitching. Take some fine rawhide lace and stitch the burner in place. Once the honda is finished, but while it's still stretched on the wooden handles, submerge it in boiling water for about one minute. The boiling water will make the rawhide extra hard. Then remove and let it dry (while stretched). You will probably want to leave it overnight or longer to get it good and dry. Once it is dry, take a very sharp knife and cut off the extra lengths. You can cut them flush with the curve of the round knot.

To attach the honda to the reata, first put a damp rag over the braid where the reata will attach. Once you can work a tool into the braid, try to find four different plaits that are in good position for a reata plait to pass

Fig. 55. A working reata that was made and is still being used by Bill Dorrance.

under. Moisten the 14-inch unbraided ends of the reata as before. Then position the honda and reata so that two strands are on one side and two on the other. Raise an appropriate strand in the honda and pass the reata strand through. The reata braid will probably require that one of these strands cross. In general, though, the look should be of parallel strands going around the honda. The four strands are then wrapped one full wrap over the reata. Then all four make a bight and return making an over one and under one pattern. Next to the honda, all four make a bight that carries them over an original strand. Then the ends are tucked up under the foundation knot. If there are five places where the weave crosses (X), then go under three and come out with all four ends 90 degrees apart. Tighten the weave by going back through your work. Make sure the honda is straight with the reata. With a smaller eye in a honda, you may have to put a slight angle to the position of the honda on the reata. Once you are done, you can cut off the extra ends.

Bill Dorrance leaves one of these ends with a length of 5 inches. Bill said this was an aid he used when working cattle alone. While on his horse, he can reach down and grab this extension to free a cow. This way the animal does not come in contact with the ends of his fingers. Thus he is less likely to get a finger caught or cause the animal to move too soon.

On the end opposite the honda, Bill usually does not do anything. As we mentioned before, the 14 to 16 inches of unbraided ends might be needed to add a honda. In Fig. 56 you can see a simple finishing of this end using a slit braid. Some braiders make this end very fancy for show or to identify their work.

These days, a good reata may last four or five years with average use, Bill speculated. He proceeded to clarify that opinion with the statement that "we're not roping as much now." In bygone days, a reata would only last him about a year. The usual procedure is to keep one reata on the saddle and two extra reatas on hand in the tack room.

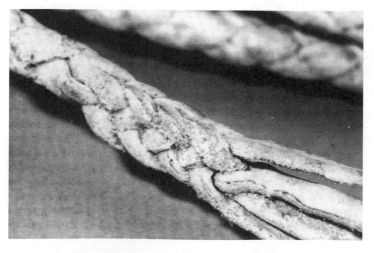

Fig. 56. The slit braid on the tail end of a reata.

11. HOBBLES

We have shown an interesting type of hobble made by Bill Dorrance and his brother in Fig. 57. This slit braid makes a very simple and functional hobble. When I first saw these, I referred to them as "rattlesnake" hobbles. I had not heard the more descriptive term of "slit braid." There are several features to these hobbles that make them very nice and easy to use. First, there are no slide knots to move. The size of the cuffs (as in "handcuffs") is smaller than most of the other hobbles shown. This tight fit and the way the slot or "eye" naturally pulls closed ensure that the hobbles do not come off accidentally. The leather skirts serve a function other than decoration: they protect the rawhide that is bending over the ring from excess moisture. Also, this fairly sharp bend of the rawhide over the ring is an area that is stronger if protected. In Fig. 58 you will see how Ernie Ladouceur carried this idea over to a more classical hobble.

Rather than spending further time on Bill's hobbles, let us go to the more classical design. The first thing you will need is a metal ring. Some people use two rings for extra strength. Bill Dorrance makes his rings out of welding rod. Just remember that a steel ring will rust. For that reason, most braiders will cover the ring with a braiding that we talked about earlier. But I have seen many fine hobbles where the ring was not covered (Fig. 59). Most of these use a solid ring that is brass plated. I recommend a 1-3/4 -inch diameter. Smaller diameters may not allow you to hang the cuffs side by side from a saddle D ring.

Next you will want to braid two lengths of eight-plait rawhide. Be sure to leave some extra unbraided length on each end. Each length of the braiding should be 32 inches long. Some hobbles even use 34 inches to give a little more distance between the horse's legs. This eight-plait can be done with or without a core, depending on your preference. If you use square reins, then you will be less interested in using a core and you will more possibly lace your work together as shown in some of the photographs.

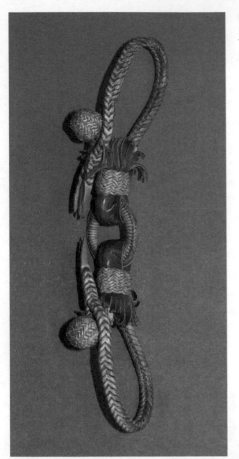

Fig. 57. Slit braid hobbies made by the late Fred Dorrance, Bill's brother. Another brother, Tom, had his work pictured in Bruce Grant's Encyclopedia of Rawhide and Leather Braiding.

Fig. 58. Hobbles by Ernie Ladouceur. These are eight plait, without a core, laced together. The leather and the six-bight knot that holds them in place have been replaced by the author.

Fig. 59. Hobbles (and part of the romal) made in 1980 by Jack Shepard for the author. Jack chose a light-colored rawhide to contrast better with the red and black. Because rawhide does not hold dyes well, I suggest that most people should use naturally colored rawhide. Leave the color complications to people who make their living with rawhide, as Jack has done for over thirty years.

Bring the two ends together and connect them in a terminal Turk's head knot as was done with the honda. This knot can now be covered with any covering knot of your choice. In Fig. 60, you will see a W, or 3-2-2-3, knot used. Probably the best choice for your first hobbles would be the first knot in this book, a six-bight ($X = 1$) with a Type 1 interweave (see chapter 5). Most hobble-covering knots are based on a six-bight knot. Do this for both braided lengths.

You now have a circle held together by your knot. Find the point on the circle that is opposite this knot. Bring that point over your knot and pull the two loops to match side by side as in Fig. 62. Open the loop and insert the ring. Arrange the knot, braiding, and ring so that they match the drawing. Where the two knots are going to be placed you will need to tie some string to temporarily hold them in the proper position. Repeat this process for both cuffs.

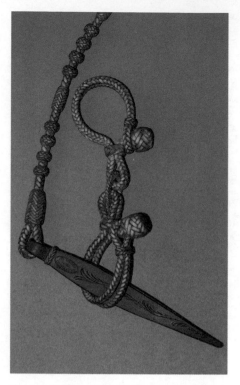

Fig. 60. Hobbles (and part of the romal) by the late Jim Shepard. Note the use of the W knot for the large round knot.

Fig. 61. Close view of a hobble knot made by Bob Stone, Woodside, California.

The stationary knots (terminal knots) that will be close to the ring can be any knot you wish. First tie a ring knot with rawhide or cover your string knot with a tape core as described in Chapter 4. Once you have your knot core, tie your knot. You might try the same knot that you used above (6 B, X = 1).

For the sliding knots (keeper knots), be sure that you have not tied your ring knot too tightly. Some braiders braid the knot over a cuff of rawhide. Probably the easiest would be to place two or four scrap pieces between the cuffs and the core knot being tied. These scraps can be removed after the finished knots dry. You can use the same covering knot at this location (6 B, X= 1).

Before you set the work aside to dry, stretch the cuffs over a soup can or other such object that is about 2-3/4 inches in diameter. Then slip the cuffs off the soup can and flatten just slightly to match the drawing. Now you can set the hobbles aside to dry. Finishing steps are described in Chapter 14.

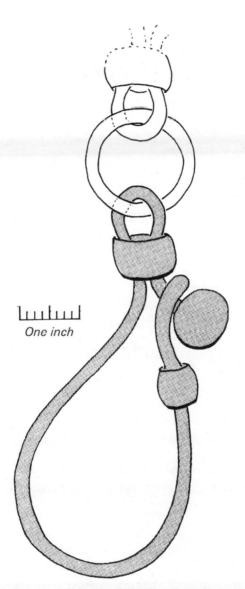

One inch

Fig. 62. Hobbles.

12. REINS AND ROMAL

Rawhide reins have more "life" than other types of reins, largely due to its material. The "feel" that the reins possess is a vital consideration in how they should be designed and made. Many very fine braiders will show off by packing as many knots onto their reins as they can. Others will try to show off by braiding large numbers of very fine plaits. But does this showing off improve the feel or usefulness of the reins? It is the author's opinion that too many knots, knots that are too long, or excessive number of plaits will all tend to destroy the flexibility of the reins. Thus they will hang wrong and not respond properly. Many of the cowboy reins are simply eight-plait without a core. These are further shaped between boards or in a vise to achieve a square cross-sectional shape. As mentioned before, this is a big help when holding reins and extra loops of reata in one hand. Also, the square shape is a more natural fit into the folds created by one's fingers. If you are using reins all day long, they just feel better.

The example shown in Fig. 63 is a twelve-plait. This is a very nice-looking braid. The beginner will probably wish to stick to an eight-plait until some experience has been gained. You can use a core in the eight-plait if you wish; just remember that you don't need extra stiffness. Make sure the core is soft and flexible. The core in this case is usually just a fine string of rawhide that is about one-third to one-half the width of the laces being used for the braiding.

The first step in braiding reins is to braid exactly 8 feet of braid. For eight-plait, try 1/8-inch-wide strings. For twelve-plait, use 3/32-inch strings. This can be with or without a core if the eight-plait is used. Make sure you have extra lengths of unbraided rawhide at each end. Tie some string around the ends to keep the braid tight. Roll, pull, or press the braiding to get the desired finish. (This is covered in more detail in Chapter 14.)

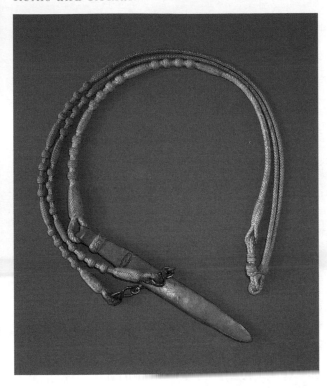

Fig. 63. Reins and romal by
Josh Chapard.

On each end, bend the end 3 inches back and tie down. Place a small length of 3/8-inch wooden dowel into the eye that you have just formed. Leave this piece of dowel there to keep the eye open.

Make sure the unbraided ends are soft enough to work. Remoisten about 2 inches of the braiding measuring from the wooden dowel. We are now ready to splice the ends into the reins. The splice is only going to be about 1-1/2 inches long. If a core has been used, you might like to remove a section of the core for this length. This can reduce the bulk created by the splice and make it easier to separate plaits for the splice. In splicing, you will work an awl into the braid to separate the plaits enough to work in the splice plaits. You will continue to weave in each of the splice plaits until you have covered about 1 /2 inch. Over the next inch you will bury one splice plait at a time. These should be staggered evenly around the remaining area so as not to cause any sudden width changes. You can hammer and roll this area to make it smooth. Then cover with one layer of tape if you wish. Over this core you will need to put a long covering knot. You can use a six-bight where X = 3. This is an area where many braiders use the multiple-string method that is used in the bosal nose button. Some of the photographs (Figs. 64,65) show a four-bight enlarged to over four. This over four uses a Type 3 for part of the interweave. Note that the top of the knot is the end away from the eye and dowel.

Now fold the rein length in half. From the end of this bight, measure back 2 inches. Here you will want a knot that is somewhat firm but which can be slid if you wish. Tie a ring knot or other type of sliding core. You may wish to use some spacers as we described under hobbles. Then cover with a knot. A good knot for this is the six-bight (X = 1) that we presented first.

Now you will be ready to put on the button knots. These can cover a length of anywhere from 16 to 22 inches. For this measurement I start from the very outside tip of the eye. I know of some braiders who use the 16- inch measure just because that is the length that one of the "masters" uses. I have also seen some very nice reins that measured to 24 inches. The work that I like the best uses a measurement of 20 inches.

Here you will have some freedom to create your own styles. I prefer to have some space between the knots. It makes the reins easier to clean. It also allows for more play or bend in reins than if the knots were stacked tight against each other. Most of the round rein buttons have about 3/8 to 1/2 inch of space between. Another way of describing this is to say that the very centers of the round knots are just short of 1 inch apart (7/8 to 15/16). In practice, what you will do is tie your first knot near the eye and dowel end. Whatever you tie on one end of the rein, try to do exactly the same to the matching other rein. In Fig. 65, there are examples of some patterns. For your first reins, try four W knots; then one 6 B, X = 2; then four W knots; then another 6 B, X = 2; four more W knots; then another 6 B, X = 2. This will complete the reins.

Fig. 64. This fancy covering on the bit end of reins was done by Jack Shepard.

Fig. 65. A four-bight (X = 2) knot with one interweave compared to a four-bight (X = 1) knot with two interweaves. Both are by Jack Shepard.

For a rein-to-romal connector, braid a length of 20 inches. Use 3/32- inch-width string in either six- or eight-plait. Connect the ends and cover with a knot like the 6 B, X = 1. This is basically the same as part of a hobbles. Two ring knots are shown in some of the examples. Other knots can be used, or you can use one knot if you wish. (In Fig. 66 I have slid the two ring knots together, but these could be replaced by one knot.) I like to open up the connector and not leave it flat as in the other photographs. With the connector's eyes open, the romal and reins have more freedom and don't get caught on the connector. You will probably find it best not to tie the sliding knots until the romal is finished and the connector is in the proper position.

The romal evolved from the quirt. Thus it could be classed as a short whip. It also serves to balance the weight of the reins. Thus if a cowboy drops his reins behind the saddle horn in order to rope or work, the reins do not fall to the ground. On the end of the quirt is a double fall, stinger, or popper. This is usually made of leather. To make the stinger, take a strip of saddle leather or belt leather that is 3/8 inch thick, 1-1/2 inches wide, and 28 inches long. The last 3 inches of the ends can be tapered to a gradual point. Fold it in half and mark off 2 inches from the fold on both sides. Trim the area between these two marks to a total width of 1 inch. Then blend the width out to the original over the next 2 inches. Set this aside for now.

Fig. 66. The rein-to-romal connector by Jack Shepard has been further opened up by the author, who feels that this personal preference helps reduce the sense of twisting or catching when in use.

For the body of the romal, you will need to have a 3-foot-long core. This will be thicker than any rein core. Most romal cores are not tapered. One-fourth inch is a good lace width. For a first project, eight-plait can be used. Once you know how to do a good job of a twelve-plait, you will probably find that the twelve-plait covers the larger diameter more nicely. Most whips use twelve-plait for the thicker parts.

Start with six strings and find the centers. Then braid 4 inches of six-plait. Bring the ends together and change to twelve-plait braid. This is where you will introduce the core. Braid for the full 3-foot length of the core. Tie some string to hold the braiding tight. Then roll, pull, or whatever method you prefer to finish the smooth round braid.

Bend the end around a 3/4-inch wooden dowel and tie it down to form an eye. Remove the dowel and slip the leather stinger in at this point. If you have the leather moist at the midpoint, the dowel can be put back in. The leather will conform to the shape of the dowel and the rawhide. Splice the unbraided ends into the romal and put a covering knot over the splice as you did for the reins. Put a six- or eight-bight knot on the stinger where the 2-inch reference mark had been made. This holds the two sides together but still allows the leather to move easily on the romal eye.

Fig. 67. The stinger, by Jack Shepard, fits on the end of the romal.

Place the romal next to the reins and copy the knots exactly as they were tied. They will be slightly larger, but they should be spaced to look the same. Up where the six-plait became the twelve, you will have to cover the changeover with whatever long knot you used in the reins.

Place the connector in the proper position and add the desired sliding knots. Attach the connector and romal to the reins and you are ready to turn to Chapter 14.

13. THE BOSAL

When a bosal is combined with a headstall, mecate, and fiador, the combination is called a hackamore. This equipment is very useful in the training of horses. Because a bit is not being used, the training does not damage or toughen the horse's mouth. Naturally, though, anything used on a horse can be misused. Thus the rider must know how to use his equipment and communicate with the horse. In most cases, if a bosal leaves the horse's nose bloody, then the rider and horse have probably been fighting, or not communicating. For different steps of training, there are different sizes of bosals. Usually the trainer will start with the largest and work down to smaller sizes. In the "Old California" style or "Spade Bit" style of training, a pencil-thick bosal is worn with the bit at all times. This reminds the horse of his previous training, helps to keep the horse's mouth closed on the bit, and can serve for a lead line. This last point is worth further discussion. Rawhide reins, or any reins, should not be used to tie a horse to a fixed object, nor should the reins be used as a lead line. The reason is that the reins are attached to the bit, and a sudden movement by the horse could cause the bit to do a lot of damage. Thus a lead line tied to a pencil-thick bosal, or the lead rope end of the mecate on a hackamore, should be used for this purpose.

Bill Dorrance tells the story of his first reins. His brother had made some rawhide reins for him. When he handed the gift to Bill, he said something like this: "If you break them in use, I'll fix them…But if you break them because you used them to tie up your horse, then you're on your own."

Bosals can be made in many sizes. Below is a listing from Jack Shepard's catalog. (Jack Shepard, who lives in Payette, Idaho, has made a living with rawhide for over 30 years. Other members of the Shepard family also make rawhide tack.) This should give you some idea of the variations that are possible. The measurement refers to diameter of the main part of the bosals.

5/16 inch:	8 plait or fancy at 12 plait
3/8 inch:	8 plait or fancy at 12 plait
1/2 inch:	8 plait or fancy at 12 plait
5/8 inch:	8 plait or fancy at 18 plait
3/4 inch:	8 plait or fancy at 18 plait
7/8 inch:	8 plait or fancy at 18 plait
1 inch:	16 plait

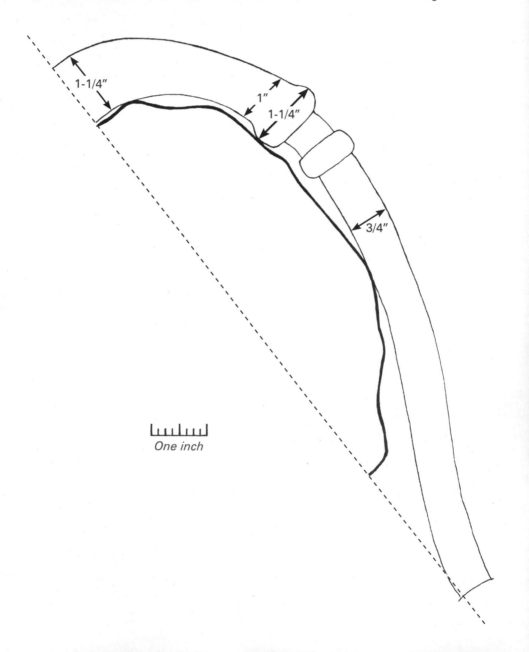

Fig. 68. A bosal.

One inch

Figs. 80 and 81 are examples of Jack Shepard's 5/16-inch pencil bosal of eight-plait. Most of the other photographs show 3/4-inch bosals.

For those wishing to try to make a bosal, I suggest that you start with the eight-plait sizes. These sizes are determined by the size of core that is used. I know of some cowboys who use different sizes of piano wire for the core. They feel that this prevents the bosal from bending where the headstall attaches. After a lot of use and some horse sweat, most bosals will show some change of shape. Sometimes a metal cable core (with a metal ring below the heel knot) is used. This type of bosal is used with a tie-down to keep the horse from throwing his head above a preset position. A very useful core is made from a section of old reata. Thus even worn-out reatas get a third life. (The first life was on the cow.) Small-diameter cores can be made by using three or four narrow strips of rawhide. These can be left straight and just held together by the braiding; probably a better way would be to tie them together on each end and in the center. Most cores that are made today are most likely twisted rawhide. By taking one or several strips of rawhide and twisting them together you can make a smooth core. You can also make a core by winding many strands together in much the same way that twisted fiber ropes are made. If this method is your choice, then start by scoring each strand down the center on the hair side of the rawhide. Then take each strand and twist it to a smooth twist. Wind one at at time, adding more strands until the desired size is reached. By alternating twist directions, some braiders intend to prevent the core from unwinding sometime in the future. Nail the strips down on each end and let them dry thoroughly. If there are some rough or irregular areas on these cores, I usually smooth them with some sandpaper after they're dry. The finished core should be at least 32 inches long.

Braid eight or more plaits over the full length of the core. In measuring a number of bosals that are pictured in this chapter, I found that 32 inches seems to be a good length. As shown in the photographs, many cowboys will not finish the bosal until it is needed; then they will be able to "custom fit" the horse. If a pencil bosal is being made then 30 inches may be long enough. If you like to tie a large knot for your mecate, then you may wish more length. The breed of horse may also make a difference.

With the braiding still out straight, find the center. From the center measure 4-3/4 to 5 inches in each direction. At these two points, tie a ring knot. You may even start your ring knot by taking the lace under one plait of the braiding. This will keep the ring knot from moving. These ring knots should be 9-1/2 to 10 inches apart. (Personal preferences influence these measurements.) In Fig. 69 there is an example of a bosal that measured 9-1/2 inches on the original nose button and was lengthened by adding extra leather ring knots. Tie two more ring knots farther from the center. There should be a space of about 3/4 inch between these knots and the first knots. These last ring knots should be left so they can be slid for adjustment. Many times they are left as such. Sometimes they are covered with a small round knot.

Fig. 69. The nose button is all herringbone on this example. Note that the nose button was short, so an extra (leather) ring knot was added.

Use some tape to build up a nice taper over the center 4 or 5 inches. This knot core and the first two ring knots will be the area covered by the nose button. In several of the examples (Figs. 70, 71, 72) we have shown the use of the gaucho weave over the ring knots and described earlier how it can be changed to the herringbone. Now cover the area with your nose button knot. Do not cut off or bury your ends yet. There are two ways to bury these ends: one would be to have them all in a line that will correspond to the inside of the bosal once it is bent into shape; the other is around the knot. Here the cut ends are located where the pattern of the braid makes its change from gaucho to herringbone. In both cases, it is best not to cut or bury your strings until after the bosal is shaped. Fig. 75 shows bosals that Bill Dorrance has waiting to be fit and finished.

Bend the two ends of the bosal together and secure with a ring knot. I prefer to use a rawhide knot but it can be tied with string first to hold the ends in place while you tie the ring knot. You can expect a couple of things to happen to the nose button with this bending. First, the braiding may bunch together some on the inside center. This will create a flat spot that will correspond to the flat area on the nose of the horse. Some braiders prefer to try to eliminate this flat area. Others look for it and like to see it; again there is a personal preference. Second, when the bosal is being shaped, you may see spaces as the knot opens up on the outside of this curve. This indicates you must re-do the knot and braid it tighter (Fig. 76). You can then bury or end your strings and smooth the knot. Some of this is described later in the chapter on finishing.

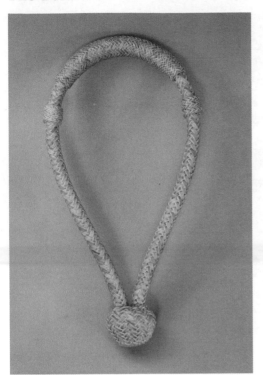

Fig. 70. A nice, typical bosal.

Fig. 71. A closer view of the nose button in Fig. 70. Note the gaucho-to-herringbone pattern that was described in the text.

Fig. 72. Another bosal with a nylon mecate (or "McCarty") ready for use.

Fig. 73. A nose button in leather being made by Gail Hought. There are small lines on the core to show the center and thus help line up the knot.

Fig. 74. The entire bosal still in production. Gail Hought used rawhide for the core; the rest of the braiding is in latigo leather.

Fig. 75. Unfinished bosals by Bill Dorrance. They will be finished to fit the horse.

Fig. 76. A close-up view of the nose button in colored leather on a bosal by Gail Hought, McKinleyville, California.

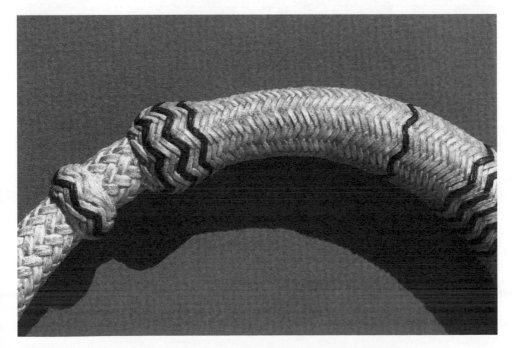

Fig. 76a. Another close-up view of a bosal, this one done by Bob Stone.

Take each rawhide string up over the ring knot and back down under the ring knot. Do this with each lace and repeat as often as is needed to fill in any spaces. We are trying to make a smooth, round, symmetrical shape as a core for a heel knot. You can get a spherical shape similar to most of the photographs or, by placing your ring knot up higher on the braid, you can get an elongated shape. Each braider has his own preferences.

Cover this with an eight-bight knot. The heel knot is where many braiders like to show their best work. Many of the fancier over four or five and under four or five patterns are used to fill in spaces created by the size and shape that you are trying to cover. Bob Stone of Woodside, California, writes, "I never know what I am going to do with a heel knot when I start it." The fancier heel knots present a challenge and an opportunity to be creative (Fig. 77).

Hang the bosal in a safe place and let it dry. Once it is dry, you can take a sharp knife and cut off the extra ends flush at the bottom. This is shown in Fig. 78. Once you have done the finishing steps mentioned in Chapter 14, you will have completed a bosal.

Fig. 77. A fancy heel knot in leather, by Gail Hought.

Fig. 78. A heel knot on a bosal by Alfredo Campos, Federal Way, Washington, showing an eight-bight knot of the simple over two, under two pattern. Note that the extra ends are cut off flush with the heel knot.

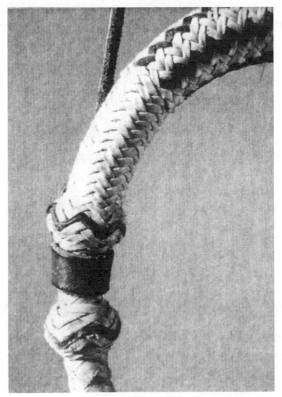

Fig. 79. This bosal uses the herringbone pattern on the ends of the nose button, and the gaucho pattern in the center.

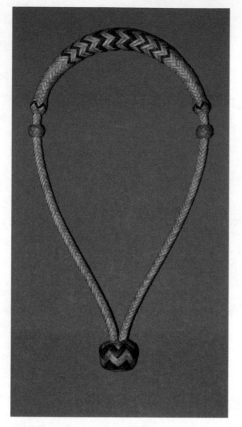

Fig. 80. A "pencil" bosal or "lead" bosal.

Fig. 81. A closer view of the heel knot by Jack Shepard, matching the reins and hobbles pictured previously. This size bosal is to be used when the horse is being ridden with bit and reins. Because no room needs to be allowed for the mecate's knot, this bosal can be slightly smaller than those shown previously.

14. FINISHING AND CARE OF FINISHED PRODUCT

There are several important considerations to be covered in this chapter. We will talk about hiding ends, smoothing the work, breaking in, care, and storage. In earlier parts of the book, we mentioned some ideas on how to bury the ends. In other places, the ends are brought up from under and just cut off flush. In the instructions, the dead end has been left at the start. In practice, you will want to withdraw the dead end and trace the pathway with the working end. Then in a convenient place (away from the edge of the knot), the dead end can be passed under at least three. The working end can complete the proper pattern before it goes under at least three other strands. The ends are pulled tight and cut off flush. If the ends are to be buried out of sight, they can be pushed under the surface of the braidwork.

Plaits can be smoothed by running the work through holes in a hardwood board. A metal tool for this purpose is shown in Fig. 52. Other methods involve rolling the work on a smooth, clean surface. A hard board or your hands can be used to put weight on your rolling efforts. One braider who was making flat braid belts and hobbles told me that he put his work in the driveway and drove his car over it. He wanted his work flat! In this book, I do not recommend that technique. When we talked about the eight-plait without a core, we mentioned the use of boards and a vise to help shape the work. The boards serve to make the vise jaws larger. The braid work is placed, pressed, rotated 90 degrees, and placed and pressed again. (It's kind of like ironing a napkin.)

By doing your shaping and finishing before the work does its final drying, you have control over the shape. If shape is very critical, allow the rawhide to dry somewhat then repeat your shaping efforts. Some items, such as twisted cores, have to be allowed to dry while being held in shape.

Buttons can be shaped and smoothed in much the same manner. If you are doing the final smoothing and your work is finished, work in some paste or glycerine type of saddle soap over all the rawhide. Then gently rub or polish your work. A piece of sheepskin (wooly side) can be used for a final buffing. Hang all work so it can dry in the desired shape.

Some old timers talk about the use of beef tallow as a surface treatment for rawhide. This would soften and waterproof the rawhide that was in daily use. Probably a lot of this just wore off quickly before it did much damage. I think that most people would be safer using only saddle soap.

Moisture, horse sweat, mold, mice, rats, horses, and other animals can all prove very dangerous to your rawhide tack. As rawhide does not take colors well, sun and use will result in the loss of colors in dyed rawhide tack. Dave Stewart suggests that any tack with strings as small as 1/16 or 1/32 of an inch are items that collectors should hang on a wall and never use. He also suggests that 1/8-inch and 3/32-inch strings are probably best for show tack that gets limited use. Dave advises that cowboy tack which is to be used should probably be made of rawhide strings that are between 5/32 and 5/16 of an inch wide. Much of the reasoning behind these choices is based on the effects of horse sweat on the finer size strings.

Gail Hought provided the following suggestions for judging work. These are all basics that you should keep in mind while working, and in evaluating what you have made.

1. Quality of the materials used.
2. Quality of the cut strings — how well they are cut and beveled.
3. Quality of the braiding:
   A. Straight plaits and knots.
   B. Correct tightness.
   C. Well-hidden ends.
4. Correct dimensions.
5. Esthetically pleasing appearance.
6. Smooth finish (unless a rough look is desired).

If your work has included some leather, you will have to be careful near the leather. Saddle soap, by itself, can be hard on leather. Neatsfoot oil, which is good for leather, can be bad for rawhide. Thus you should soap and clean the leather first, then oil and polish the leather without getting any oil on the rawhide. Finally, you can put saddle soap on the rawhide. If a little gets on the leather, buff it off quickly. The oils in the leather will protect it from a little saddle soap — in fact, a very light coat of saddle soap can be buffed to a nice polish.

Reins should always be hung at the rein-to-romal connector. This will allow them to hang straight when not being used. If you use rein chains, you might wish to use a clip on the end to allow for easy removal of the bit from the reins. If you have your rein chains attached to the bit in a fixed manner, then you will have to hang the reins and bridle so that the chains are slack and there is no extra weight on the reins. Besides this advantage to rein chains, they protect the rawhide from the horse's saliva.

Reatas and reins will feel better once they have been broken in. To do this, you just need to use them some. Unless you use a Mexican saddle or wrap your horn so that it is about 6 inches in diameter, you will not be able to take proper dallies with your reata. The horns on most new western saddles are not designed for rawhide. Taking rawhide dallies on a small diameter horn is not good for the reata.

Other suggestions for care of rawhide tack are that you keep the items in a dry, clean, lighted storage area. Damp and dark areas are good places for mold, not rawhide. Metal containers or rope-carrying containers may be good for keeping rats and mice away from your good show reatas. One caution is that the reata might rub against the metal and get a metal-colored deposit on the rub spot.

If you clean and take care of your rawhide tack, it will last a long time and give you good service. There is a lot of work involved in braiding rawhide. Thus, my final piece of advice is that you stop and rest if you feel you are getting tired. You will not do good work if you keep working past the point at which you should have stopped.

For those of you who decide to work with rawhide, practice and experience will be the greatest teachers. You will be following in the footsteps of many, many generations. Without question, rawhide is the fiber of the Old West.

A Bridge from Past to Present

For the purposes of this book and to help the beginner to "not get lost," most of the patterns presented have the second pass close to the first pass, etc. Once one really gets into braiding, the multi-string approach becomes the standard. Many will develop their own patterns, starting in the middle of the lace to form a foundation by working one direction and then doing the interweave in the opposite direction.

I have not gone into much detail concerning color interweaves since I personally prefer the pattern changes when working in rawhide. The truth is that rawhide is not a color-stable material. Over the past thirty years, I have seen all of the colored rawhide samples fade. Even the Kangaroo lacing on my fid has deteriorated or faded greatly. I was told years ago by an old braider that he had a black formula that did not fade, but that he could no longer get that dye — that was back in the 1970s. Red is a color that quickly fades in the work of all the braiders that would discuss their attempts and failures.

For the sake of disclosure, all of the color images included in this edition are from slides of photographs I took thirty years ago. These can be used along with the original photos and material presented in the first edition. I told the "story" years ago that I had written the book so that I could re-teach myself the art of braiding when I retired. Well, after practicing dentistry for forty years, I now find myself having to re-read my own book for a different reason — the opportunity to include some of the material that was edited from the original.

As I write this closing, I am reminded of one of my young patients from about fifteen years ago who told me how he had learned from my book years before, and had bought a new copy so he could get back into braiding — and here I thought I was the one that would be using the book to "get back into braiding." You just never know to whom or how far away one's influence will extend. Thirty years ago I contemplated the concern that the best hides for rawhide came from a cow that had starved to death: the supply was becoming practically non-existent. Today I contemplate how modern computers and digital photography have left the "old ways" in the dust. How long will there be people interested in carrying on this "bunk-house," time-consuming, "busy work"? Can they spend enough time away from the TV or computer to it carry on? On the other hand, I ended the text in the first edition with a statement that "rawhide is the fiber of the Old West." Now, thirty years later, I must say that my vision has expanded. Even if only as a decoration, rawhide braiding has a fascination worldwide that serves as a small "window" connecting the past to the future.

Drawings and Instructions on Various Interweave Patterns

Over the years, some of the comments that have gotten back to me concern the "W knot" on page 61. Please remember that rawhide is NOT like braiding leather, Kangaroo lace, or rope. Rawhide does best when the bights are NOT sharp. I found a similar knot in my notes and present it here for the reader to experiment with on their own.

"Cowboy" Round Rein Button
Using Only One Length Of Lace

PASS (A = DOWN / B = UP)			INSTRUCTIONS = OVER OR UNDER	
1. A.	Down & Up & Down. This last down is parallel and tight against the left edge of the standing end (the start).			
B.	The first Under will be at the first bottom Bight			U1
2. A.				U1
B.				U1
3. A.				U2
B.				U2
4. A.				U3
B.				U3
5. A.				U3
B.	O1			U3
6. A.	O1			U3
B.	O2			U3
7. A.	O2			U3
B.	O2	U1		U3
8. A.	O2	U1		U3
B.	O2	U2		U3
9. A.	O2	U2		U3
B.	O2	U2	O1	U3
10. A.	O2	U2	O1	U3
B.	O2	U2	O2	U3
11. A.	O2	U2	O2	U3
B.	O2	U2	O2	U3
12. A.	O2	U2	O2	U3
B.	O2	U2	O2	U3

APPENDIX A

2013

In the thirty years since the research for this book was first started, additional material has been gathered. Since the whole idea of the book was to share information, the re-printing of the book provides an opportunity to share some of these additional ideas, photos, and examples. I have received communications from all over the world and have heard that the book has been used to help in a wide range of activities, from rehabilitation to serving as a college text. I hope that the additional materials help to re-energize the interest in this most fascinating use of human creativity.

Flat Start to Knots

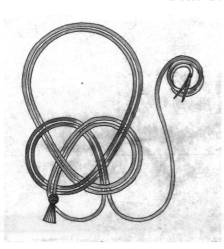

Because the Alamar was a popular parade decoration in the Salinas Rodeo Parade back when I wrote the book, I studied the several patterns that were used to tie this Hair Rope. Once the nationwide professionals replaced the local participants in the Rodeo, the local characteristics and even the track event for "best working tack" quickly became a thing of the past. Now the Alamar is not seen in the Pre-Rodeo Parade. Originally the hair rope was used in the training of young horses by teaching the horse to pay attention to the hair "reins" on the neck. The California style of horse training starts by using a large Bosal, moving to smaller Bosals, down to a "Pencil Bosal" along with a bit, and finally to a bit without a Bosal. Thus for a parade, the rider is "showing off" that his horse no longer needs the earlier steps of training.

In the late 1970s to the early 1980s, it was becoming difficult to find someone who remembered how to tie the Alamar properly. Many locals just slipped the entire tied Alamar over the horse's head and saved it for another parade, rather than using the hair rope with the bosal, and carrying it as an Alamar, to keep the hair rope available if needed. After talking to some who did know how to tie the knot correctly, I realized that it was just a flat version of the Four Bight Turk's Head Knot. It was this realization that prompted me to decide that the easiest way to start most knots is with an "OVER." Back when I wrote the book, I used an Apple II computer. Below are some drawings that I produced at that time:

Four Bight Turk's Head Knot

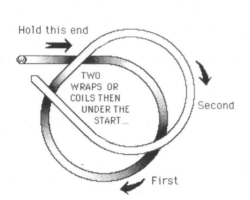

Hold this end

TWO WRAPS OR COILS THEN UNDER THE START...

Second

First

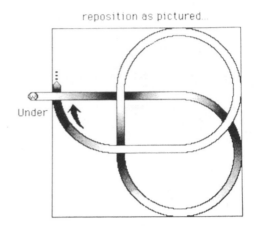

reposition as pictured...

Under

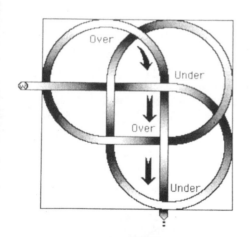

Over

Under

Over

Under

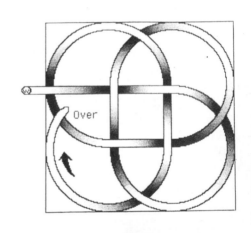

Over

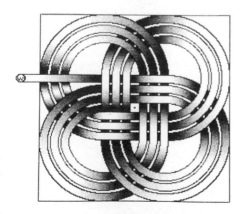

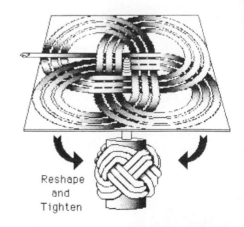

Reshape and Tighten

Fig. 82.

Five Bight Turks Head Knot

OVER ONE

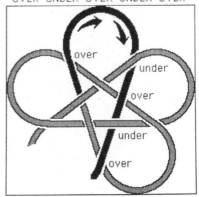

OVER-OVER-OVER-UNDER

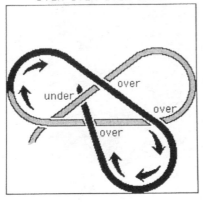

OVER-UNDER-OVER-UNDER-OVER

RESHAPE OVER CENTER DOWEL

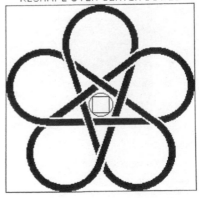

Examples Best Told in Photos

Expanding on the idea of "sharing examples," we show Figure 83. You might recognize this as being on Page 86. I show it here to represent the Four Plait braid Reata. Figure 84 shows an Eight Plait Reata using a center core so that the braid is "round" rather than "square" in cross section. Unfortunately, I have lost reference to the maker, but I believe it was Bob Stone. Figures 85 and 86 are of a Six Plait Reata by Bill Radcliffe of Carmel Valley, California. This dates from about 1940.

Fig. 83

Fig. 84

Fig. 85

Fig. 86

The Knot Roundups
From Page to Knot

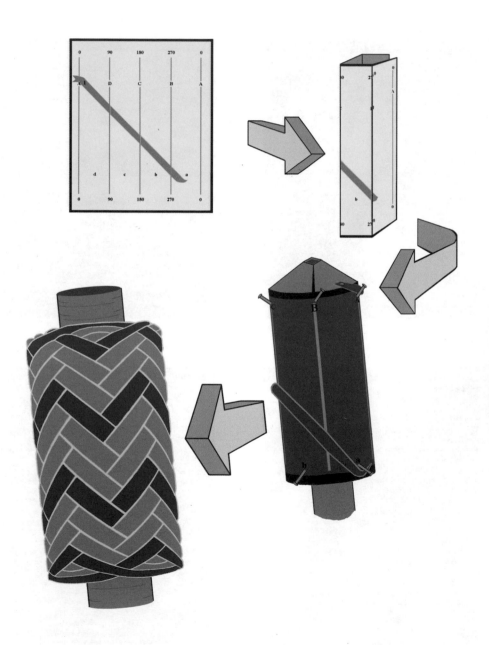

Instructions for Four-Bight Knot
Based on Over Three & Under Three

STEP	PASS	INSTRUCTIONS = OVER OR UNDER
1	1. A.	From Pin "A" to around Pin "a" for first Bight
2	B.	- - - - - - - - - O - - - - - -
3	2. A.	- - - - - - - - - O - - - - - -
4	B.	U - - - - - - - - O - - U - - -
5	3. A.	U - - - - - - - - O - - U - - -
6	B.	U - - O - - - - - O - - U - - O
7	4. A.	U - - O - - - - - O - - U - - O
8	B.	U - - O - - U - - O - - U - - O
9	5. A.	- O - - U - - O - - U - - O - - U
10	B.	U - - O - - U - - O O - U - - O -
11	6. A.	- O - - U - - O - O U - - O - - U
12	B.	U U - O - - U - - O O - U U - O -
13	7. A.	U O - - U - - O - O U - U O - - U
14	B.	U U - O O - U - - O O - U U - O O
15	8. A.	U O - O U - - O - O U - U O - O U
16	B.	U U - O O - U U - O O - U U - O O
17	9. A.	- - O O - U U - O O - U U - O O - U U - O O
18	B.	- - O O - U U - O O O U U - O O - U U O O O
19	10. A.	- - O O - U U - O O O U U - O O - U U O O O
20	B.	- - O O U U U O O O U U - O O - U U U O O O
21	11. A.	- O O - U U - O O O U U - O O - U U - O O O
22	B.	- O O - U U U O O O U U - O O - U U U O O O
23	12. A.	- O O O U U U O O O U U - O O O U U U O O O
24	B.	- O O O U U U O O O U U - O O - U U U O O O
25	13. A.	- O O O U U U O O O U U U O O O U U U O O O
26	B.	U O O O U U U O O O U U U O O O U U U O O O

STEP 1 FOUNDATION

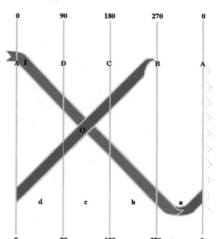

STEP 2 FOUNDATION

STEP 3 FOUNDATION

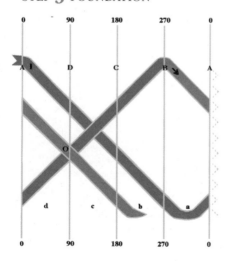

STEP 4 FOUNDATION

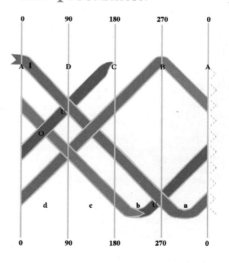

STEP 5 FOUNDATION

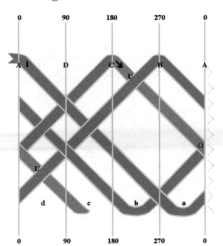

STEP 6 FOUNDATION

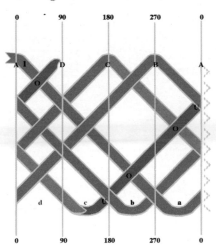

STEP 7 FOUNDATION

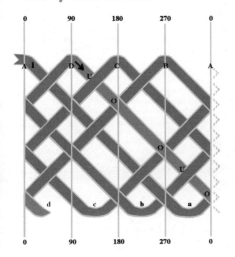

STEP 8 FOUNDATION

Second Interweave to Third

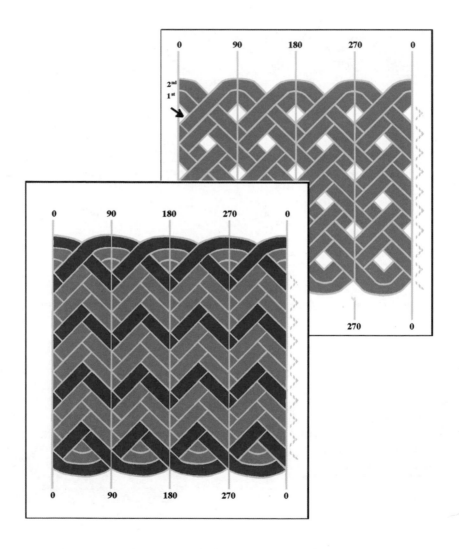

STEP **9** SECOND INTERWEAVE

STEP **10**

STEP **11**

STEP **12**

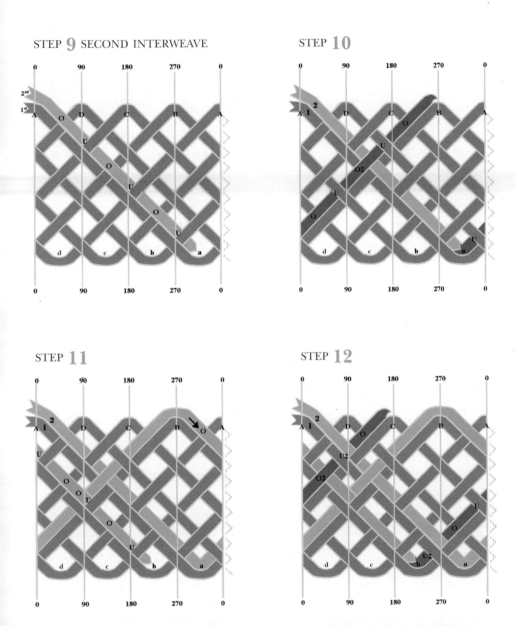

STEP **13**

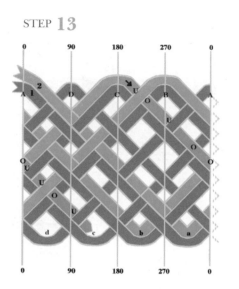

STEP **14**

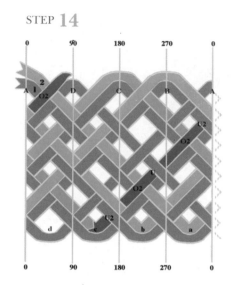

STEP **15**

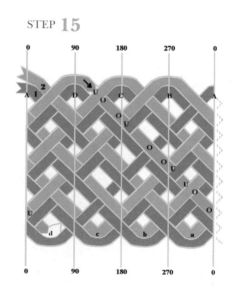

STEP **16**

STEP **17**

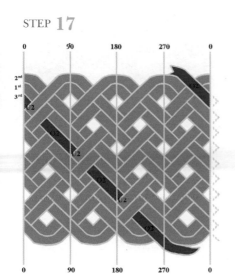

STEP **18**

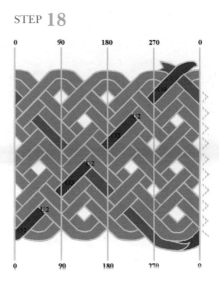

STEP **19**

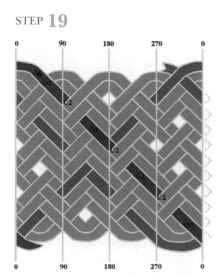

STEP **20**

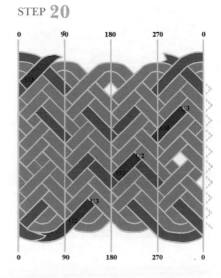

STEP **21**

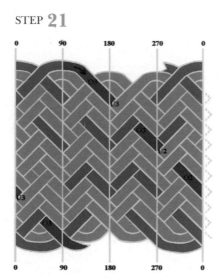

STEP **22**

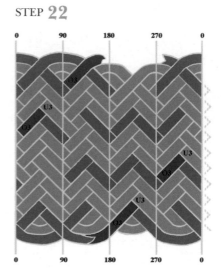

STEP **23**

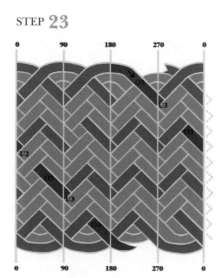

STEP **24**

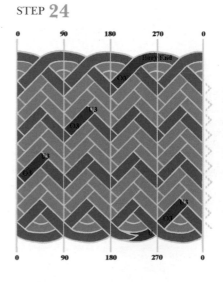

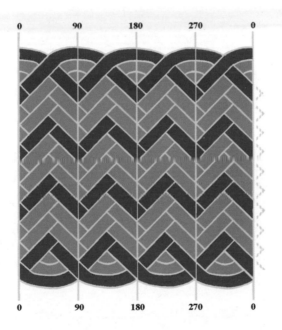

0   90   180   270   0

0   90   180   270   0

Now, try to expand on, and apply,
everything presented in an eight bight
using six rings of color.

Instructions for EIGHT Bight with Six Rings of Color
NOTE: * INDICATES CAUTION AS "OVER" FOLLOWS "OVER"

PASS A = DOWN B = UP	INSTRUCTIONS = OVER OR UNDER	
1. A.		
B.	O	
2. A.	O	
B.	U	O U
3. A.	U	O U
B.	U O *	O U O
4. A.	U O *	O U O
B.	U O U	O U O U
5. A.	U O U	O U O U
B.	U O U O *	O U O U O
6. A.	U O U O *	O U O U O
B.	U O U O U	O U O U O U
7. A.	U O U O U	O U O U O U
B.	U O U O U O *	O U O U O U O
8. A.	U O U O U O *	O U O U O U O
B.	U O U O U O U	O U O U O U O...

•Interweave or add color
•Start between 1 & 8 by under two

PASS												
9. A.	O	U	O	U	O	U	O	U	O	U	O	U2
B.	O	U	O	U	O	U	O2	U	O	U	O	U2
10. A.	O	U	O	U	O	U	O2	U	O	U	O	U2
B.	O	U2	O	U	O	U	O2	U	O	U2	O	U2
11. A.	O	U2	O	U	O	U	O2	U	O	U2	O	U2
B.	O	U2	O	U	O2	U	O2	U	O	U2	O	U2
12. A.	O	U2	O	U	O2	U	O2	U	O	U2	O	U3
B.	O	U2	O	U	O2	U	O2	U2	O	U2	O	U3
13. A.	O	U2	O	U	O2	U	O2	U2	O	U2	O	U3
B.	O	U2	O2	U	O2	U	O2	U2	O	U2	O2	U3
14. A.	O	U2	O2	U	O2	U	O2	U2	O	U2	O2	U3
B.	O	U2	O2	U	O2	U2	O2	U2	O	U2	O2	U3
15. A.	O	U2	O2	U	O2	U2	O2	U2	O	U2	O2	U3
B.	O2	U2	O2	U	O2	U2	O2	U2	O2	U2	O2	U3
16. A.	O2	U2	O2	U	O2	U2	O2	U2	O2	U2	O2	U3
B.	O2	U2	O2	U2	O2	U2	O2	U2	O2	U2	O2	U=end

COMBINATION KNOT

Gaucho – to – Herringbone – to – Gaucho

Instructions for Combination Knot Using Only One Length of Lace:
Gaucho – to – Herringbone – to – Gaucho

PASS	A = DOWN B = UP	INSTRUCTIONS = OVER OR UNDER	
1. A.	Clockwise wrap	
B.	X Cross two times	
	Tight against the start then:	
2. A.	U1	U1
B.	O1, U1	U1, O1
3. A.	O2	U2
B.	U2, O1	U1, O2
4. A.	O1, U2	O1, U2
B.	U1, O2, U1	U2, O2
5. A.	U2, O2	O2, U2
B.	O2, U2, O1	O1, U2, O2
6. A.	U1, O2, U2	U1, O2, U2
B.	U3, O2, U1	O2, U2, O2
7. A.	O2, U2, O2	U2, O2, U2
B.	O1, U1, O2, U2, O1	U1, O2, U2, O2
8. A.	U1, O1, U1, O2, U2	O1, U2, O2, U2
B.	O2, U3, O2, U1	U2, O2, U2, O2
9. A.	U2, O2, U2, O2	U1, O1, U2, O2, U2
B.	U1, O2, U1, O2, U2, O1	O2, U1, O2, U2, O2
10. A.	O1, U2, O1, U1, O2, U2	U1, O2, U2, O2, U2
B.	U2, O2, U3, O2, U1	O1, U3, O2, U2, O2
11. A.	O2, U2, O2, U2, O2	O2, U1, O1, U2, O2, U2
B.	O1, U2, O2, U1, O2, U2, O1	U2, O2, U1, O2, U2, O2
12. A.	U1, O2, U2, O1, U1, O2, U2	O1, U2, O2, U2, O2, U2
B.	O2, U2, O2, U3, O2, U2, O2, U3, O2, U2, O2	

Combination Knot
PASS 1

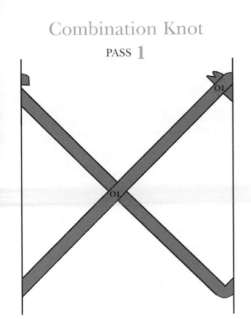

Combination Knot
PASS 2

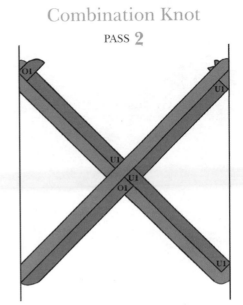

Combination Knot
PASS 3

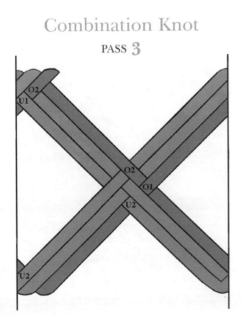

Combination Knot
PASS 4

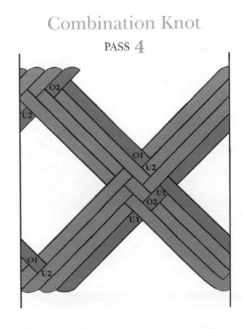

Combination Knot
PASS 5

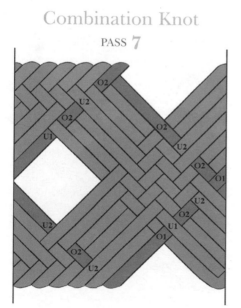

Combination Knot
PASS 6

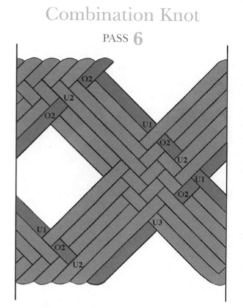

Combination Knot
PASS 7

Combination Knot
PASS 8

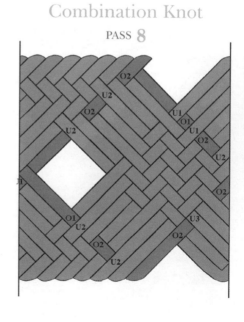

Combination Knot
PASS 9

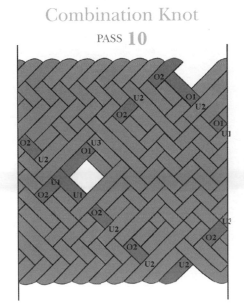

Combination Knot
PASS 10

Combination Knot
PASS 11

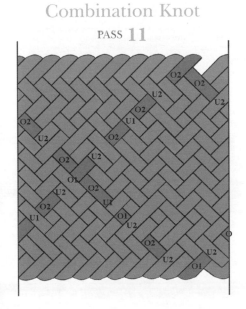

Combination Knot
PASS 12

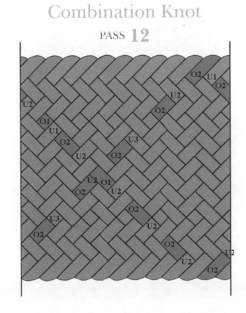

APPENDIX B

The following plates are from Bruce Grant's
Encyclopedia of Rawhide and Leather Braiding,
copyright © 1972 by Cornell Maritime Press, Inc., by permission.

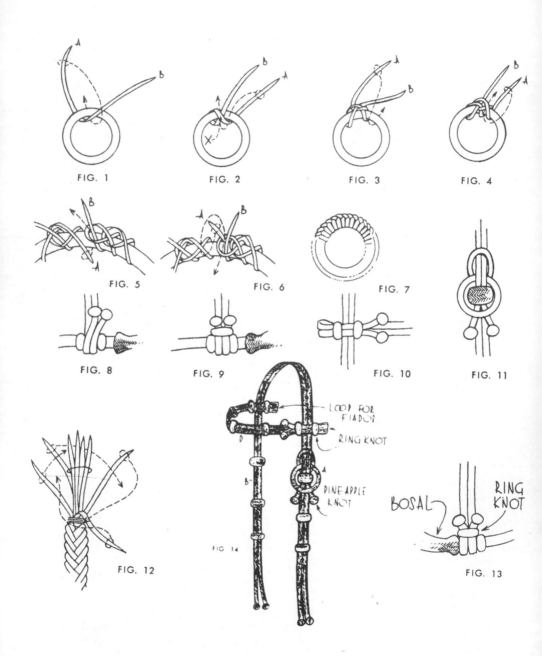

FIG. 1   FIG. 2   FIG. 3   FIG. 4

FIG. 5   FIG. 6   FIG. 7   FIG. 11

FIG. 8   FIG. 9   FIG. 10

LOOP FOR FIADOR

RING KNOT

PINEAPPLE KNOT

FIG. 12   FIG 14   BOSAL   RING KNOT

FIG. 13

PLATE 52. How to Make a Braided Hackamore Headstall.

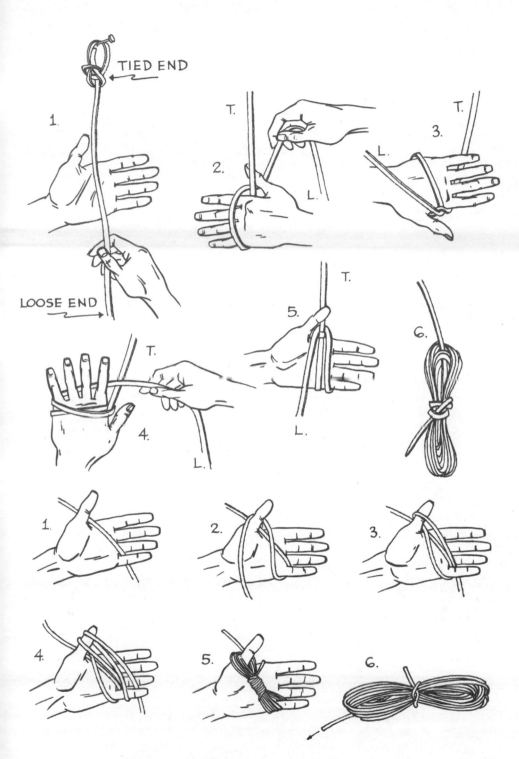

PLATE 76. How to Make the Tamale.

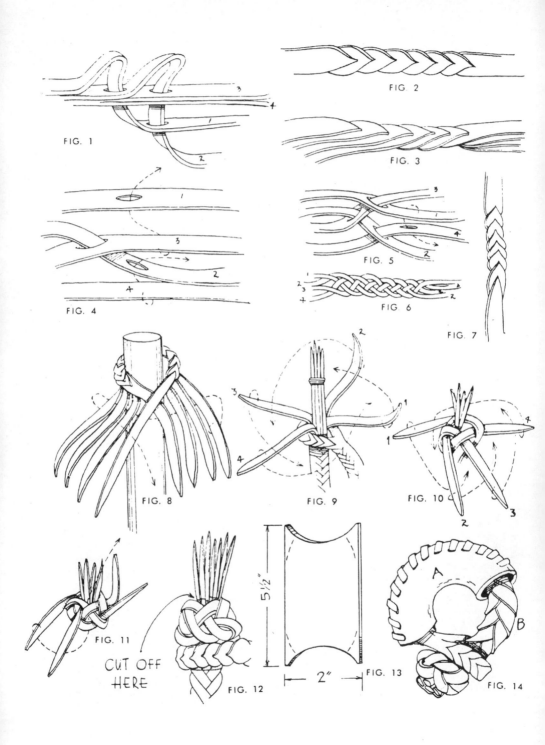

PLATE 78. How to Make a San J nan Honda.

GALLERY

With this edition, we will try to
expand on the fancier patterns that
are possible with braiding. Again,
there is great value in just seeing
examples in order to find what one
likes or does not like.

Sample of various patterns and sizes with knots on Rawhide Reins

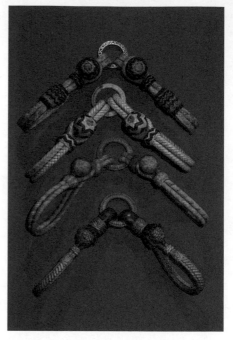

Sample of various patterns with knots on Rawhide Hobbles

Close-up of pattern on commercial Rawhide Reins by Jack Shepard

Close-up of pattern on commercial Rawhide Reins

Rawhide Bosal

Rawhide Bosal. See the close-up in Figure 79 on page 109.

This work was by Gail Hought and dates from 1984.

 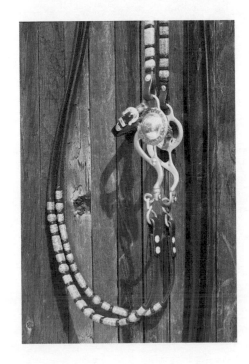

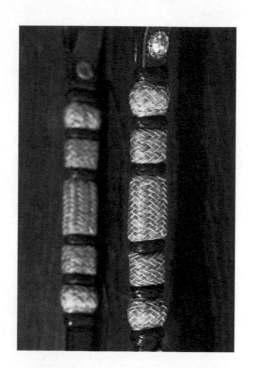

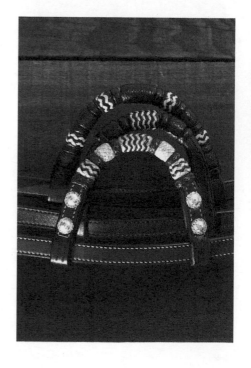

This work, by David L. Stewart, is noted as "16 string of 5/8 inch with 40 and 60 string nose button."

Close-up of this same work by David L. Stewart, 1984.

Hobbles by Bob Stone, 1984.

Close-up of work by Bob Stone, 1984.

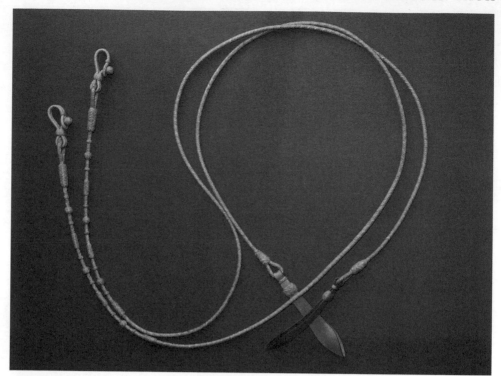

Reins Close by Bob Stone, 1984.

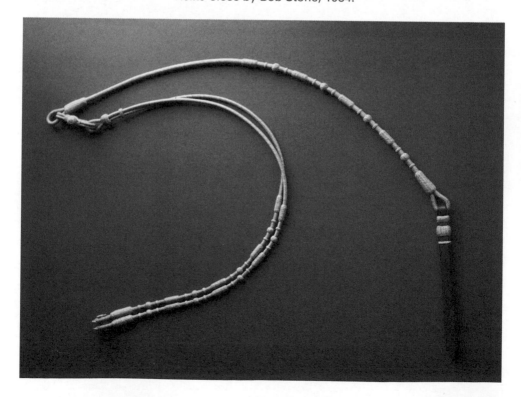

An "FID" sent to the author as a gift from Ed Pass of Australia

These examples of work by Ed Pass demonstrate the quality of kangaroo lace.

Hubbles by Bob Kelley, photo from August 1981. (Also see top picture on next page.)

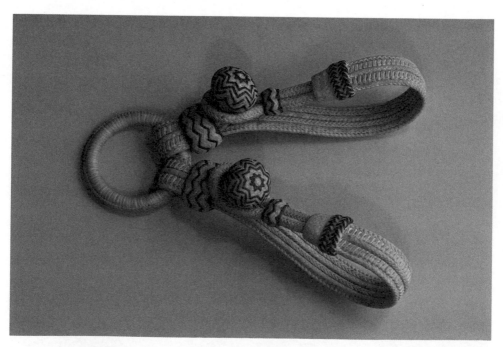

Hobbles by Bob Stone, photo taken February 1988.

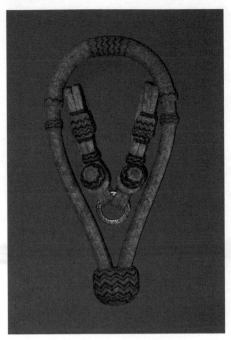

Hobbles and Bosal by Bob Stone.

This is a rawhide "Sampler" made as a Show Dog Leash. It was custom-made by Bob Stone for the author, who used it when showing his Newfoundland Dog, "Nick," in obedience competitions.

Nylon Hobbles with Rawhide Buttons made by Loren Wood of Oregon. The nylon cording is very strong and not prone to stretching if it gets moist from rain or dew on grass.

Hobbles made about twenty-three years ago by the late M. A. Bardoff of Idaho.

Hobbles made by Frank Hansen.

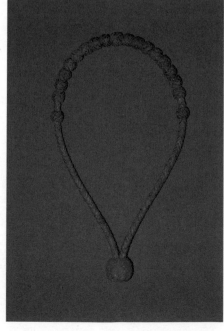

Pencil Bosal showing individual nose button knots.

Figure 60 on page 92.

Figure 80 on page 110.

Figure 59 on page 91.

Tribute to Bill Dorrance

Much of the inspiration for this book came from knowing the late Bill Dorrance. This inspiration actually went both ways. By seeing his work being published in magazines and in this book, he proceeded to write his own book on how to train horses. Below is a collection of photos that did not make it into the original text.

Bill Dorrance demonstrating throwing a reata: May 1980, Salinas, California

Bill Dorrance leaves a length of rawhide near the Honda to help prevent getting any fingers caught when freeing the caught cow or calf

Bill Dorrance demonstrating
at his work bench

Bill hard at work.

Similar to Figure 19 on page 35.

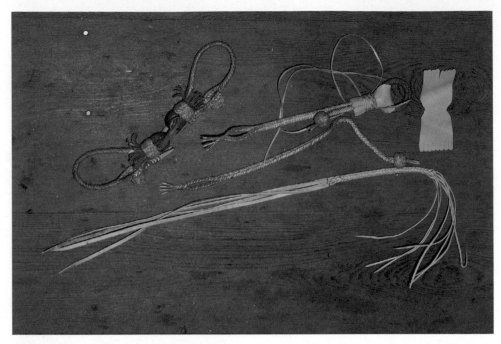

Bill Dorrance had these unfinished hobbles in various stages of construction.

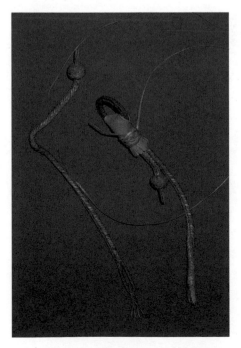

Bill Dorrance had these unfinished hobbles in various stages of construction.

Compare to Figure 57 on page 90.

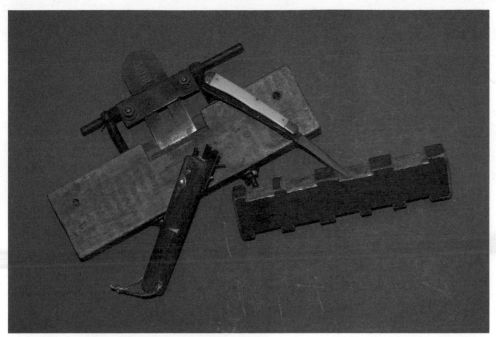

Compare to Figures 8 and 9 on page 21.

Other tools used by Bill Dorrance.

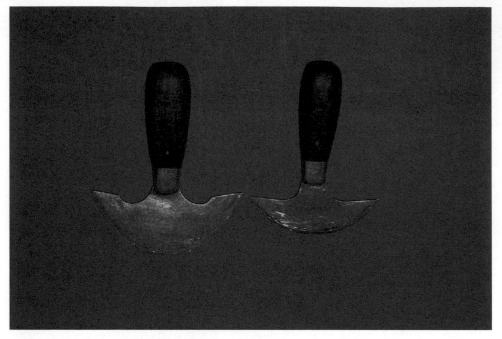

Other tools used by Bill Dorrance; these show the changes from use and sharpening.

Bill Dorrance's tack room in April of 1981.

Bill Dorrance's saddle, showing the "Old California" style horn and wrap.

Bill Dorrance at a Branding: labeled "underhand throw," photo dated 1968.

Bill Dorrance demonstrating the use of a reata: May 1980, Salinas, California.

Bill Dorrance demonstrating "freeing a reata": May 1980, Salinas, California.

RECOMMENDED READING

Grant, Bruce. *Encyclopedia of Rawhide and Leather Braiding*. Centreville, Maryland: Cornell Maritime Press, 1972.

Graumont, Raoul, and John Hensel. *Encyclopedia of Knots and Fancy Rope Work, Fourth Edition*. Centreville, Maryland: Cornell Maritime Press, 1952.

Morgan, David W. *Whips and Whipmaking: With a Practical Introduction to Braiding*. Centreville, Maryland: Cornell Maritime Press, 1972.

INDEX

INDEX B

Made by Gail Hought.